DIET SMOOTHIES FOR
WEIGHT LOSS

DROOL WITH SMOOTHIES

50 Smoothie Recipes For Detox and Weight Loss

TAYLOR UNDERWOOD

Copyright © 2020 Taylor Underwood

All Rights Reserved

Copyright 2020 By Taylor Underwood - All rights reserved.

The following book is produced below with the goal of providing information that is as accurate and reliable as possible. Regardless, purchasing this book can be seen as consent to the fact that both the publisher and the author of this book are in no way experts on the topics discussed within and that any recommendations or suggestions that are made herein are for entertainment purposes only. Professionals should be consulted as needed prior to undertaking any of the action endorsed herein.

This declaration is deemed fair and valid by both the American Bar Association and the Committee of Publishers Association and is legally binding throughout the United States.

Furthermore, the transmission, duplication or reproduction of any of the following work including specific information will be considered an illegal act irrespective of if it is done electronically or in print. This extends to creating a secondary or tertiary copy of the work or a recorded copy and is only allowed with express written consent from the Publisher. All additional right reserved.

The information in the following pages is broadly considered to be a truthful and accurate account of facts and as such any inattention, use or misuse of the information in question by the reader will render any resulting actions solely under their purview. There are no scenarios in which the publisher or the original author of this work can be in any fashion deemed liable for any hardship or damages that may befall them after undertaking information described herein.

Additionally, the information in the following pages is intended only for informational purposes and should thus be thought of as universal. As befitting its nature, it is presented without assurance regarding its prolonged validity or interim quality. Trademarks that are mentioned are done without written consent and can in no way be considered an endorsement from the trademark holder.

Table of Contents

PART I 13

Smoothie Diet Recipes 14

    Chapter 1: Fruit Smoothies 15

        Quick Fruit Smoothie 15

        Triple Threat Smoothie 17

        Tropical Smoothie 18

        Fruit and Mint Smoothie 19

        Banana Smoothie 21

        Dragon Fruit Smoothie 23

        Kefir Blueberry Smoothie 25

        Ginger Fruit Smoothie 27

        Fruit Batido 29

        Banana Peanut Butter Smoothie 30

    Chapter 2: Breakfast Smoothies 31

        Berry Banana Smoothie 31

        Berry Surprise 32

        Coconut Matcha Smoothie 34

        Cantaloupe Frenzy 35

        Berry Lemon Smoothie 36

        Orange Glorious 38

        Grapefruit Smoothie 39

        Sour Smoothie 40

        Ginger Orange Smoothie 41

        Cranberry Smoothie 42

Creamsicle Smoothie 44

Sunshine Smoothie 45

Chapter 3: Vegetable Smoothies 46

Mango Kale Berry Smoothie 46

Breakfast Pink Smoothie 47

Butternut Squash Smoothie 49

Zucchini and Wild Blueberry Smoothie 50

Cauliflower and Blueberry Smoothie 51

Immunity Booster Smoothie 52

Ginger, Carrot, and Turmeric Smoothie 54

Romaine Mango Smoothie 56

Fig Zucchini Smoothie 57

Carrot Peach Smoothie 58

Sweet Potato and Mango Smoothie 60

Carrot Cake Smoothie 61

Chapter 4: Green Smoothies 62

Kale Avocado Smoothie 62

Celery Pineapple Smoothie 64

Cucumber Mango and Lime Smoothie 65

Kale, Melon, and Broccoli Smoothie 67

Kiwi Spinach Smoothie 69

Avocado Smoothie 70

PART II 72

Chapter 1: Meal Planning 101 73

Make a Menu 74

Plan around Ads 74

Go Meatless Once Per Week 74

Use Ingredients That You Already Have On Hand 75

Avoid Recipes that Call for a Special Ingredient 75

Use Seasonal Foods.. 75

Make Use of Leftovers and Extra Portions 76

Eat What You Enjoy.. 76

Chapter 2: 1 Month Meal Plan.. 77

Week 1: Success is no accident—you have to reach for it 77

Mediterranean Breakfast Sandwich.. 77

Greek Chicken Bowls 79

Ratatouille.. 81

Snack Platter.. 83

Week 2: Self-belief and effort will take you to what you want to achieve
.... 86

Breakfast Quesadilla.. 86

Greek Orzo Salad... 87

One Pot Mediterranean Chicken... 89

Mediterranean Nachos 91

Week 3: The harder you work, the greater the success........................... 92

Breakfast Tostadas 92

Roasted Vegetable Bowl.. 93

Mediterranean Chicken... 95

Baked Phyllo Chips 97

Week 4: You don't need perfection—you need effort 98

Mini Omelets... 98

Basil Shrimp Salad.. 100

Mediterranean Flounder... 101

Nutty Energy Bites 103

Week 5: Transformation Happens One Day at a Time 105

Mediterranean Breakfast Bowl 105

Chicken Shawarma Pita Pockets 107

Turkey Mediterranean Casserole 108

Heirloom Tomato and Cucumber Toast 110

Chapter 3: Maintaining Your Diet 111

Find Your Motivation 111

Remind Yourself Why You are Eating Healthily 112

Eat Slowly 112

Keep Yourself Accountable 113

Remember Your Moderation 114

Identify the Difference between Hunger and Craving 114

Stick to the Meal Plan 115

Drink Plenty of Water 115

Eat Several Times Per Day 116

Fill Up on Protein 116

Keep Only Healthy Foods 117

Eat Breakfast Daily 117

PART III 119

Chapter 1: Identifying the Mediterranean Diet 120

Defining the Mediterranean Lifestyle 121

The Rules of the Mediterranean Diet 122

Chapter 2: Savory Mediterranean Meals 125

Mediterranean Feta Mac and Cheese 125

Chickpea Stew 125

Savory Mediterranean Breakfast Muffins 126

Mediterranean Breakfast Bake 127

Mediterranean Pastry Pinwheels 129

Chapter 3: Sweet Treats on the Mediterranean Diet 131

Greek Yogurt Parfait 131

Overnight Oats 132

Apple Whipped Yogurt 133

Chapter 4: Gourmet Meals on the Mediterranean Diet 134

Garlic-Roasted Salmon and Brussels Sprouts 134

Walnut Crusted Salmon with Rosemary 135

Spaghetti and Clams 136

Braised Lamb and Fennel 137

Mediterranean Cod 139

Baked Feta with Olive Tapenade 140

Chapter 5: 30-Minutes or Less Meals 141

Vegetarian Toss Together Mediterranean Pasta Salad 141

Vegetarian Aglio e Olio and Broccoli 142

Cilantro and Garlic Baked Salmon 143

Harissa Pasta 144

1 Hour Baked Cod 145

Grilled Chicken Mediterranean Salad 146

Lemon Herb Chicken and Potatoes One Pot Meal 148

Vegetarian Mediterranean Quiche 150

Herbed Lamb and Veggies 151

Chicken and Couscous Mediterranean Wraps 152

Sheet Pan Shrimp 154

Mediterranean Mahi Mahi 156

Chapter 7: Slow Cooker Meals 157

Slow Cooker Mediterranean Chicken 157

Slow Cooker Vegetarian Mediterranean Stew 159

Vegetarian Slow Cooker Quinoa..161

Slow-Cooked Chicken and Chickpea Soup...163

Slow Cooked Brisket...165

Vegan Bean Soup with Spinach 166

Moroccan Lentil Soup 167

Chapter 8: Vegetarian and Vegan Meals 169

Vegetarian Greek Stuffed Mushrooms 169

Vegetarian Cheesy Artichoke and Spinach Stuffed Squash...................170

Vegan Mediterranean Buddha Bowl 172

Vegan Mediterranean Pasta 174

Vegetarian Zucchini Lasagna Rolls 176

Vegetarian Breakfast Sandwich 177

Vegan Breakfast Toast 179

Vegetarian Shakshouka 180

PART IV 182

Chapter 1: The Fundamentals of a Low Sugar Diet for Diabetics 183

Chapter 2: Benefits of a Low Sugar Diet for Diabetics 186

Chapter 3: Savory Recipe Ideas 189

Savory Idea #1: Tangy Cabbage Treat...189

Savory Idea #2: Low-carb Egg &Veggie Bites 191

Savory Idea #3: Yummy Chicken Dee-light 193

Savory Idea #4: Low-carb Fried Chicken Surprise 195

Savory Idea #5: Low-Sugar Beef Explosion 197

Savory Idea #6: Tangy Pork Extravaganza 199

Savory Idea #7: Filet & Cheese Supreme 201

Savory Idea #8: Quick and Easy Low-carb Chips 202

Savory Idea #9: Unbelievably Low-carb South Treat 203

Savory Idea #10: Low-sugar Italian Snack Option 205

Chapter 4: Gourmet Recipe Ideas 207

Gourmet Idea #1: Tasty Chicken and Veggie Pot 207

Gourmet Idea #2: Delicious Low-sugar Chicken Meal 208

Gourmet Idea #3: Italian Chicken Dinner Delight 210

Gourmet Idea #4: Yummy Lemon Beef Surprise 212

Gourmet Idea #5: Gourmet Sirloin Option 213

Gourmet Idea #6: Unbelievably Low-sugar Surprise 215

Gourmet Idea #7: Low-carb Salmon Delight 216

Gourmet Idea #8: Shrimp-Avocado Treat 218

Gourmet Idea #9: Gourmet Hot Pot Surprise 219

Gourmet Idea #10: Low-carb Tuna Wraps Treat 220

Chapter 5: Quick and Easy Recipe Ideas 221

Quick and Easy Idea #1: Quick and Easy Veggie Treat 221

Quick and Easy Idea #2: Spicy Egg and Veggie Dash 223

Quick and Easy Idea #3: Low-sugar Hot Cake Surprise 224

Quick and Easy Idea #4: Cheesy Veggie Bites 226

Quick and Easy Idea #5: Low-carb Pudding Dee-light 228

Quick and Easy Idea #6: Tangy Egg Salad 229

Quick and Easy Idea #7: Cheesy Egg Cups 231

Quick and Easy Idea #8: Asparagus Appetizer/Side Salad 233

Quick and Easy Idea #9: Low-carb Pork Treat 234

Quick and Easy Idea #10: Easy Fish Delight 235

Chapter 6: Low-Carb Recipe Ideas 236

    Low-Carb Recipe Idea #1: Balsamic Roast Delight............................236

    Low-Carb Recipe Idea #2: Burger Calzone Treat 238

    Low-Carb Recipe Idea #3: Steak Skillet Nacho 240

    Low-Carb Recipe Idea #4: Portobello Burger Meal 242

    Low-Carb Recipe Idea #5: Low-carb Super Chili.................................244

    Low-Carb Recipe Idea #6: "You won't believe it's low-carb" Chicken Parmesan 245

    Low-Carb Recipe Idea #7: Tangy Coconut Chicken 247

    Low-Carb Recipe Idea #8: Slow cook Chicken Casserole....................250

    Low-Carb Recipe Idea #9: Low-carb Roll Up Treat 251

    Low-Carb Recipe Idea #10: Cauliflower Cheese Surprise....................252

Chapter 7: 7-day Sample Low Sugar Diet Plan... 253

PART I

Smoothie Diet Recipes

The smoothie diet is all about replacing some of your meals with smoothies that are loaded with veggies and fruits. It has been found that the smoothie diet is very helpful in losing weight along with excess fat. The ingredients of the smoothies will vary, but they will focus mainly on vegetables and fruits. The best part about the smoothie diet is that there is no need to count your calorie intake and less food tracking. The diet is very low in calories and is also loaded with phytonutrients.

Apart from weight loss, there are various other benefits of the smoothie diet. It can help you to stay full for a longer time as most smoothies are rich in fiber. It can also help you to control your cravings as smoothies are full of flavor and nutrients. Whenever you feel like snacking, just prepare a smoothie, and you are good to go. Also, smoothies can aid in digestion as they are rich in important minerals and vitamins. Fruits such as mango are rich in carotenoids that can help in improving your skin quality. As the smoothie diet is mainly based on veggies and fruits, it can detoxify your body.

In this section, you will find various recipes of smoothies that you can include in your smoothie diet.

Chapter 1: Fruit Smoothies

The best way of having fruits is by making smoothies. Fruit smoothies can help you start your day with loads of nutrients so that you can remain energetic throughout the day. Here are some easy-to-make fruit smoothie recipes that you can enjoy during any time of the day.

Quick Fruit Smoothie

Total Prep & Cooking Time: Fifteen minutes

Yields: Four servings

Nutrition Facts: Calories: 115.2 | Protein: 1.2g | Carbs: 27.2g | Fat: 0.5g | Fiber: 3.6g

Ingredients

- One cup of strawberries
- One banana (cut in chunks)
- Two peaches
- Two cups of ice
- One cup of orange and mango juice

Method:

1. Add banana, strawberries, and peaches in a blender.
2. Blend until frothy and smooth.
3. Add the orange and mango juice and blend again. Add ice for adjusting the consistency and blend for two minutes.
4. Divide the smoothie in glasses and serve with mango chunks from the top.

Triple Threat Smoothie

Total Prep & Cooking Time: Ten minutes

Yields: Four servings

Nutrition Facts: Calories: 132.2 | Protein: 3.4g | Carbs: 27.6g | Fat: 1.3g | Fiber: 2.7g

Ingredients

- One kiwi (sliced)
- One banana (chopped)
- One cup of each
  - Ice cubes
  - Strawberries
- Half cup of blueberries
- One-third cup of orange juice
- Eight ounces of peach yogurt

Method:

1. Add kiwi, strawberries, and bananas in a food processor.
2. Blend until smooth.
3. Add the blueberries along with orange juice. Blend again for two minutes.
4. Add peach yogurt and ice cubes. Give it a pulse.
5. Pour the prepared smoothie in smoothie glasses and serve with blueberry chunks from the top.

Tropical Smoothie

Total Prep & Cooking Time: Fifteen minutes

Yields: Two servings

Nutrition Facts: Calories: 127.3 | Protein: 1.6g | Carbs: 30.5g | Fat: 0.7g | Fiber: 4.2g

Ingredients

- One mango (seeded)
- One papaya (cubed)
- Half cup of strawberries
- One-third cup of orange juice
- Five ice cubes

Method:

1. Add mango, strawberries, and papaya in a blender. Blend the ingredients until smooth.
2. Add ice cubes and orange juice for adjusting the consistency.
3. Blend again.
4. Serve with strawberry chunks from the top.

Fruit and Mint Smoothie

Total Prep & Cooking Time: Fifteen minutes

Yields: Two servings

Nutrition Facts: Calories: 90.3 | Protein: 0.7g | Carbs: 21.4g | Fat: 0.4g | Fiber: 2.5g

Ingredients

- One-fourth cup of each
    - Applesauce (unsweetened)
    - Red grapes (seedless, frozen)
- One tbsp. of lime juice
- Three strawberries (frozen)
- One cup of pineapple cubes
- Three mint leaves

Method:

1. Add grapes, lime juice, and applesauce in a blender. Blend the ingredients until frothy and smooth.

2. Add pineapple cubes, mint leaves, and frozen strawberries in the blender. Pulse the ingredients for a few times until the pineapple and strawberries are crushed.

3. Serve with mint leaves from the top.

Banana Smoothie

Total Prep & Cooking Time: Ten minutes

Yields: Four servings

Nutrition Facts: Calories: 122.6 | Protein: 1.3g | Carbs: 34.6g | Fat: 0.4g | Fiber: 2.2g

Ingredients

- Three bananas (sliced)
- One cup of fresh pineapple juice
- One tbsp. of honey
- Eight cubes of ice

Method:

1. Combine the bananas and pineapple juice in a blender.
2. Blend until smooth.
3. Add ice cubes along with honey.
4. Blend for two minutes.
5. Serve immediately.

Dragon Fruit Smoothie

Total Prep & Cooking Time: Twenty minutes

Yields: Four servings

Nutrition Facts: Calories: 147.6 | Protein: 5.2g | Carbs: 21.4g | Fat: 6.4g | Fiber: 2.9g

Ingredients

- One-fourth cup of almonds
- Two tbsps. of shredded coconut
- One tsp. of chocolate chips
- One cup of yogurt
- One dragon fruit (chopped)
- Half cup of pineapple cubes
- One tbsp. of honey

Method:

1. Add almonds, dragon fruit, coconut, and chocolate chips in a high power blender. Blend until smooth.
2. Add yogurt, pineapple, and honey. Blend well.
3. Serve with chunks of dragon fruit from the top.

Kefir Blueberry Smoothie

Total Prep & Cooking Time: Fifteen minutes

Yields: Two servings

Nutrition Facts: Calories: 304.2 | Protein: 7.3g | Carbs: 41.3g | Fat: 13.2g | Fiber: 4.6g

Ingredients

- Half cup of kefir
- One cup of blueberries (frozen)
- Half banana (cubed)

- One tbsp. of almond butter
- Two tsps. of honey

Method:

1. Add blueberries, banana cubes, and kefir in a blender.
2. Blend until smooth.
3. Add honey and almond butter.
4. Pulse the smoothie for a few times.
5. Serve immediately.

Ginger Fruit Smoothie

Total Prep & Cooking Time: Fifteen minutes

Yields: Two servings

Nutrition Facts: Calories: 160.2 | Protein: 1.9g | Carbs: 41.3g | Fat: 0.7g | Fiber: 5.6g

Ingredients

- One-fourth cup of each
    - Blueberries (frozen)
    - Green grapes (seedless)
- Half cup of green apple (chopped)
- One cup of water
- Three strawberries
- One piece of ginger
- One tbsp. of agave nectar

Method:

1. Add blueberries, grapes, and water in a blender. Blend the ingredients.
2. Add green apple, strawberries, agave nectar, and ginger. Blend for making thick slushy.
3. Serve immediately.

Fruit Batido

Total Prep & Cooking Time: Fifteen minutes

Yields: Six servings

Nutrition Facts: Calories: 129.3 | Protein: 4.2g | Carbs: 17.6g | Fat: 4.6g | Fiber: 0.6g

Ingredients

- One can of evaporated milk
- One cup of papaya (chopped)
- One-fourth cup of white sugar
- One tsp. of vanilla extract
- One tsp. of cinnamon (ground)
- One tray of ice cubes

Method:

1. Add papaya, white sugar, cinnamon, and vanilla extract in a food processor. Blend the ingredients until smooth.
2. Add milk and ice cubes. Blend for making slushy.
3. Serve immediately.

Banana Peanut Butter Smoothie

Total Prep & Cooking Time: Ten minutes

Yields: Four servings

Nutrition Facts: Calories: 332 | Protein: 13.2g | Carbs: 35.3g | Fat: 17.8g | Fiber: 3.9g

Ingredients

- Two bananas (cubed)
- Two cups of milk
- Half cup of peanut butter
- Two tbsps. of honey
- Two cups of ice cubes

Method:

1. Add banana cubes and peanut butter in a blender. Blend for making a smooth paste.
2. Add milk, ice cubes, and honey. Blend the ingredients until smooth.
3. Serve with banana chunks from the top.

Chapter 2: Breakfast Smoothies

Smoothie forms an essential part of breakfast in the smoothie diet plan. Here are some breakfast smoothie recipes for you that can be included in your daily breakfast plan.

Berry Banana Smoothie

Total Prep & Cooking Time: Twenty minutes

Yields: Two servings

Nutrition Facts: Calories: 330 | Protein: 6.7g | Carbs: 56.3g | Fat: 13.2g | Fiber: 5.5g

Ingredients

- One cup of each
    - Strawberries
    - Peaches (cubed)
    - Apples (cubed)
- One banana (cubed)
- Two cups of vanilla ice cream
- Half cup of ice cubes
- One-third cup of milk

Method:

1. Place strawberries, peaches, banana, and apples in a blender. Pulse the ingredients.
2. Add milk, ice cream, and ice cubes. Blend the smoothie until frothy and smooth.
3. Serve with a scoop of ice cream from the top.

Berry Surprise

Total Prep & Cooking Time: Ten minutes

Yields: Two servings

Nutrition Facts: Calories: 164.2 | Protein: 1.2g | Carbs: 40.2g | Fat: 0.4g | Fiber: 4.8g

Ingredients

- One cup of strawberries
- Half cup of pineapple cubes
- One-third cup of raspberries
- Two tbsps. of limeade concentrate (frozen)

Method:

1. Combine pineapple cubes, strawberries, and raspberries in a food processor. Blend the ingredients until smooth.
2. Add the frozen limeade and blend again.
3. Divide the smoothie in glasses and serve immediately.

Coconut Matcha Smoothie

Total Prep & Cooking Time: Twenty minutes

Yields: Two servings

Nutrition Facts: Calories: 362 | Protein: 7.2g | Carbs: 70.1g | Fat: 8.7g | Fiber: 12.1g

Ingredients

- One large banana
- One cup of frozen mango cubes
- Two leaves of kale (torn)
- Three tbsps. of white beans (drained)
- Two tbsps. of shredded coconut (unsweetened)
- Half tsp. of matcha green tea (powder)
- Half cup of water

Method:

1. Add cubes of mango, banana, white beans, and kale in a blender. Blend all the ingredients until frothy and smooth.

2. Add shredded coconut, white beans, water, and green tea powder. Blend for thirty seconds.

3. Serve with shredded coconut from the top.

Cantaloupe Frenzy

Total Prep & Cooking Time: Ten minutes

Yields: Three servings

Nutrition Facts: Calories: 108.3 | Protein: 1.6g | Carbs: 26.2g | Fat: 0.2g | Fiber: 1.6g

Ingredients

- One cantaloupe (seeded, chopped)
- Three tbsps. of white sugar
- Two cups of ice cubes

Method:

1. Place the chopped cantaloupe along with white sugar in a blender. Puree the mixture.
2. Add cubes of ice and blend again.
3. Pour the smoothie in serving glasses. Serve immediately.

Berry Lemon Smoothie

Total Prep & Cooking Time: Ten minutes

Yields: Four servings

Nutrition Facts: Calories: 97.2 | Protein: 5.4g | Carbs: 19.4g | Fat: 0.4g | Fiber: 1.8g

Ingredients

- Eight ounces of blueberry yogurt
- One and a half cup of milk (skim)
- One cup of ice cubes
- Half cup of blueberries
- One-third cup of strawberries
- One tsp. of lemonade mix

Method:

1. Add blueberry yogurt, skim milk, blueberries, and strawberries in a food processor. Blend the ingredients until smooth.
2. Add lemonade mix and ice cubes. Pulse the mixture for making a creamy and smooth smoothie.
3. Divide the smoothie in glasses and serve.

Orange Glorious

Total Prep & Cooking Time: Ten minutes

Yields: Four servings

Nutrition Facts: Calories: 212 | Protein: 3.4g | Carbs: 47.3g | Fat: 1.5g | Fiber: 0.5g

Ingredients

- Six ounces of orange juice concentrate (frozen)
- One cup of each
    - Water
    - Milk
- Half cup of white sugar
- Twelve ice cubes
- One tsp. of vanilla extract

Method:

1. Combine orange juice concentrate, white sugar, milk, and water in a blender.
2. Add vanilla extract and ice cubes. Blend the mixture until smooth.
3. Pour the smoothie in glasses and enjoy!

Grapefruit Smoothie

Total Prep & Cooking Time: Ten minutes

Yields: Two servings

Nutrition Facts: Calories: 200.3 | Protein: 4.7g | Carbs: 46.3g | Fat: 1.2g | Fiber: 7.6g

Ingredients

- Three grapefruits (peeled)
- One cup of water
- Three ounces of spinach
- Six ice cubes
- Half-inch piece of ginger
- One tsp. of flax seeds

Method:

1. Combine spinach, grapefruit, and ginger in a high power blender. Blend until smooth.
2. Add water, flax seeds, and ice cubes. Blend smooth.
3. Pour the smoothie in glasses and serve.

Sour Smoothie

Total Prep & Cooking Time: Ten minutes

Yields: Two servings

Nutrition Facts: Calories: 102.6 | Protein: 2.3g | Carbs: 30.2g | Fat: 0.7g | Fiber: 7.9g

Ingredients

- One cup of ice cubes
- Two fruit limes (peeled)
- One orange (peeled)
- One lemon (peeled)
- One kiwi (peeled)
- One tsp. of honey

Method:

1. Add fruit limes, lemon, orange, and kiwi in a food processor. Blend until frothy and smooth.
2. Add cubes of ice and honey. Pulse the ingredients.
3. Divide the smoothie in glasses and enjoy!

Ginger Orange Smoothie

Total Prep & Cooking Time: Ten minutes

Yields: One serving

Nutrition Facts: Calories: 115.6 | Protein: 2.2g | Carbs: 27.6g | Fat: 1.3g | Fiber: 5.7g

Ingredients

- One large orange
- Two carrots (peeled, cut in chunks)
- Half cup of each
    - Red grapes
    - Ice cubes
- One-fourth cup of water
- One-inch piece of ginger

Method:

1. Combine carrots, grapes, and orange in a high power blender. Blend until frothy and smooth.
2. Add ice cubes, ginger, and water. Blend the ingredients for thirty seconds.
3. Serve immediately.

Cranberry Smoothie

Total Prep & Cooking Time: One hour and ten minutes

Yields: Two servings

Nutrition Facts: Calories: 155.9 | Protein: 2.2g | Carbs: 33.8g | Fat: 1.6g | Fiber: 5.2g

Ingredients

- One cup of almond milk
- Half cup of mixed berries (frozen)
- One-third cup of cranberries
- One banana

Method:

1. Blend mixed berries, banana, and cranberries in a high power food processor. Blend until smooth.

2. Add almond milk and blend again for twenty seconds.

3. Refrigerate the prepared smoothie for one hour.

4. Serve chilled.

Creamsicle Smoothie

Total Prep & Cooking Time: Ten minutes

Yields: Two servings

Nutrition Facts: Calories: 121.3 | Protein: 4.7g | Carbs: 19.8g | Fat: 2.5g | Fiber: 0.3g

Ingredients

- One cup of orange juice
- One and a half cup of crushed ice
- Half cup of milk
- One tsp. of white sugar

Method:

1. Blend milk, orange juice, white sugar, and ice in a high power blender.
2. Keep blending until there is no large chunk of ice. Try to keep the consistency of slushy.
3. Serve immediately.

Sunshine Smoothie

Total Prep & Cooking Time: Thirty minutes

Yields: Four servings

Nutrition Facts: Calories: 176.8 | Protein: 4.2g | Carbs: 39.9g | Fat: 1.3g | Fiber: 3.9g

Ingredients

- Two nectarines (pitted, quartered)
- One banana (cut in chunks)
- One orange (peeled, quartered)
- One cup of vanilla yogurt
- One-third cup of orange juice
- One tbsp. of honey

Method:

1. Add banana chunks, nectarines, and orange in a blender. Blender for two minutes.
2. Add vanilla yogurt, honey, and orange juice. Blend the ingredients until frothy and smooth.
3. Pour the smoothie in glasses and serve.

Chapter 3: Vegetable Smoothies

Apart from fruit smoothies, vegetable smoothies can also provide you with essential nutrients. In fact, vegetable smoothies are tasty as well. So, here are some vegetable smoothie recipes for you.

Mango Kale Berry Smoothie

Total Prep & Cooking Time: Ten minutes

Yields: Four servings

Nutrition Facts: Calories: 117.3 | Protein: 3.1g | Carbs: 22.6g | Fat: 3.6g | Fiber: 6.2g

Ingredients

- One cup of orange juice
- One-third cup of kale
- One and a half cup of mixed berries (frozen)
- Half cup of mango chunks
- One-fourth cup of water
- Two tbsps. of chia seeds

Method:

1. Take a high power blender and add kale, orange juice, berries, mango chunks, chia seeds, and half a cup of water.

2. Blend the ingredients on high settings until smooth.

3. In case the smoothie is very thick, you can adjust the consistency by adding more water.

4. Pour the smoothie in glasses and serve.

Breakfast Pink Smoothie

Total Prep & Cooking Time: Ten minutes

Yields: Two servings

Nutrition Facts: Calories: 198.3 | Protein: 12.3g | Carbs: 6.3g | Fat: 4.5g | Fiber: 8.8g

Ingredients

- One and a half cup of strawberries (frozen)
- One cup of raspberries
- One orange (peeled)

- Two carrots
- Two cups of coconut milk (light)
- One small beet (quartered)

Method:

1. Add strawberries, raspberries, and orange in a blender. Blend until frothy and smooth.

2. Add beet, carrots, and coconut milk.

3. Blend again for one minute.

4. Divide the smoothie in glasses and serve.

Butternut Squash Smoothie

Total Prep & Cooking Time: Five minutes

Yields: Four servings

Nutrition Facts: Calories: 127.3 | Protein: 2.3g | Carbs: 32.1g | Fat: 1.2g | Fiber: 0.6g

Ingredients

- Two cups of almond milk
- One-fourth cup of nut butter (of your choice)
- One cup of water
- One and a half cup of butternut squash (frozen)
- Two ripe bananas
- One tsp. of cinnamon (ground)
- Two tbsps. of hemp protein
- Half cup of strawberries
- One tbsp. of chia seeds
- Half tbsp. of bee pollen

Method:

1. Add butternut squash, bananas, strawberries, and almond milk in a blender. Blend until frothy and smooth.
2. Add water, nut butter, cinnamon, hemp protein, chia seeds, and bee pollen. Blend the ingredients f0r two minutes.
3. Divide the smoothie in glasses and enjoy!

Zucchini and Wild Blueberry Smoothie

Total Prep & Cooking Time: Ten minutes

Yields: Three servings

Nutrition Facts: Calories: 190.2 | Protein: 7.3g | Carbs: 27.6g | Fat: 8.1g | Fiber: 5.7g

Ingredients

- One banana
- One cup of wild blueberries (frozen)
- One-fourth cup of peas (frozen)
- Half cup of zucchini (frozen, chopped)
- One tbsp. of each
    - Hemp hearts
    - Chia seeds
    - Bee pollen
- One-third cup of almond milk
- Two tbsps. of nut butter (of your choice)
- Ten cubes of ice

Method:

1. Add blueberries, banana, peas, and zucchini in a high power blender. Blend the ingredients for two minutes.

2. Add chia seeds, hemp hearts, almond milk, bee pollen, nut butter, and ice. Blend the mixture for making a thick and smooth smoothie.

3. Pour the smoothie in glasses and serve with chopped blueberries from the top.

Cauliflower and Blueberry Smoothie

Total Prep & Cooking Time: Five minutes

Yields: Two servings

Nutrition Facts: Calories: 201.9 | Protein: 7.1g | Carbs: 32.9g | Fat: 10.3g | Fiber: 4.6g

Ingredients

- One Clementine (peeled)
- Three-fourth cup of cauliflower (frozen)
- Half cup of wild blueberries (frozen)
- One cup of Greek yogurt
- One tbsp. of peanut butter
- Bunch of spinach

Method:

1. Add cauliflower, Clementine, and blueberries in a blender. Blend for one minute.
2. Add peanut butter, spinach, and yogurt. Pulse the ingredients for two minutes until smooth.
3. Divide the prepared smoothie in glasses and enjoy!

Immunity Booster Smoothie

Total Prep & Cooking Time: Ten minutes

Yields: Two servings

Nutrition Facts: Calories: 301.9 | Protein: 5.4g | Carbs: 70.7g | Fat: 4.3g | Fiber: 8.9g

Ingredients

For the orange layer:

- One persimmon (quartered)
- One ripe mango (chopped)
- One lime (juiced)
- One tbsp. of nut butter (of your choice)
- Half tsp. of turmeric powder
- One pinch of cayenne pepper
- One cup of coconut milk

For the pink layer:

- One small beet (cubed)
- One cup of berries (frozen)
- One pink grapefruit (quartered)
- One-fourth cup of pomegranate juice
- Half cup of water
- Six leaves of mint
- One tsp. of honey

Method:

1. Add the ingredients for the orange layer in a blender. Blend for making a smooth liquid.
2. Pour the orange liquid evenly in serving glasses.
3. Add the pink layer ingredients in a blender. Blend for making a smooth liquid.
4. Pour the pink liquid slowly over the orange layer.
5. Pour in such a way so that both layers can be differentiated.
6. Serve immediately.

Ginger, Carrot, and Turmeric Smoothie

Total Prep & Cooking Time: Forty minutes

Yields: Two servings

Nutrition Facts: Calories: 140 | Protein: 2.6g | Carbs: 30.2g | Fat: 2.2g | Fiber: 5.6g

Ingredients

For carrot juice:

- Two cups of water
- Two and a half cups of carrots

For smoothie:

- One ripe banana (sliced)
- One cup of pineapple (frozen, cubed)
- Half tbsp. of ginger
- One-fourth tsp. of turmeric (ground)
- Half cup of carrot juice
- One tbsp. of lemon juice
- One-third cup of almond milk

Method:

1. Add water and carrots in a high power blender. Blend on high settings for making smooth juice.

2. Take a dish towel and strain the juice over a bowl. Squeeze the towel for taking out most of the juice.

3. Add the ingredients for the smoothie in a blender and blend until frothy and creamy.

4. Add carrot juice and blend again.

5. Pour the smoothie in glasses and serve.

Romaine Mango Smoothie

Total Prep & Cooking Time: Five minutes

Yields: Two servings

Nutrition Facts: Calories: 117.3 | Protein: 2.6g | Carbs: 30.2g | Fat: 0.9g | Fiber: 4.2g

Ingredients

- Sixteen ounces of coconut water
- Two mangoes (pitted)
- One head of romaine (chopped)
- One banana
- One orange (peeled)
- Two cups of ice

Method:

1. Add mango, romaine, orange, and banana in a high power blender. Blend the ingredients until frothy and smooth.
2. Add coconut water and ice cubes. Blend for one minute.
3. Pour the prepared smoothie in glasses and serve.

Fig Zucchini Smoothie

Total Prep & Cooking Time: Ten minutes

Yields: Two servings

Nutrition Facts: Calories: 243.3 | Protein: 14.4g | Carbs: 74.3g | Fat: 27.6g | Fiber: 9.3g

Ingredients

- Half cup of cashew nuts
- One tsp. of cinnamon (ground)
- Two figs (halved)
- One banana
- Half tsp. of ginger (minced)
- One-third tsp. of honey
- One-fourth cup of ice cubes
- One pinch of salt
- Two tsps. of vanilla extract
- Three-fourth cup of water
- One cup of zucchini (chopped)

Method:

1. Add all the listed ingredients in a high power blender. Blend for two minutes until creamy and smooth.
2. Pour the smoothie in serving glasses and serve.

Carrot Peach Smoothie

Total Prep & Cooking Time: Ten minutes

Yields: Two servings

Nutrition Facts: Calories: 191.2 | Protein: 11.2g | Carbs: 34.6g | Fat: 2.7g | Fiber: 5.4g

Ingredients

- Two cups of peach
- One cup of baby carrots
- One banana (frozen)
- Two tbsps. of Greek yogurt
- One and a half cup of coconut water
- One tbsp. of honey

Method:

1. Add peach, baby carrots, and banana in a high power blender. Blend on high settings for one minute.
2. Add Greek yogurt, honey, and coconut water. Give the mixture a whizz.
3. Pour the smoothie in glasses and serve.

Sweet Potato and Mango Smoothie

Total Prep & Cooking Time: Ten minutes

Yields: Two servings

Nutrition Facts: Calories: 133.3 | Protein: 3.6g | Carbs: 28.6g | Fat: 1.3g | Fiber: 6.2g

Ingredients

- One small sweet potato (cooked, smashed)
- Half cup of mango chunks (frozen)
- Two cups of coconut milk
- One tbsp. of chia seeds
- Two tsps. of maple syrup
- A handful of ice cubes

Method:

1. Add mango chunks and sweet potato in a high power blender. Blend until frothy and smooth.
2. Add chia seeds, coconut milk, ice cubes, and maple syrup. Blend again for one minute.
3. Divide the smoothie in glasses and serve.

Carrot Cake Smoothie

Total Prep & Cooking Time: Ten minutes

Yields: Two servings

Nutrition Facts: Calories: 289.3 | Protein: 3.6g | Carbs: 47.8g | Fat: 1.3g | Fiber: 0.6g

Ingredients

- One cup of carrots (chopped)
- One banana
- Half cup of almond milk
- One cup of Greek yogurt
- One tbsp. of maple syrup
- One tsp. of cinnamon (ground)
- One-fourth tsp. of nutmeg
- Half tsp. of ginger (ground)
- A handful of ice cubes

Method

1. Add banana, carrots, and almond milk in a blender. Blend until frothy and smooth.

2. Add yogurt, cinnamon, maple syrup, ginger, nutmeg, and ice cubes. Blend again for two minutes.

3. Divide the smoothie in serving glasses and serve.

Notes:

- You can add more ice cubes and turn the smoothie into slushy.
- You can store the leftover smoothie in the freezer for two days.

Chapter 4: Green Smoothies

Green smoothies can help in the process of detoxification as well as weight loss. Here are some easy-to-make green smoothie recipes for you.

Kale Avocado Smoothie

Total Prep & Cooking Time: Ten minutes

Yields: Two servings

Nutrition Facts: Calories: 401 | Protein: 11.2g | Carbs: 64.6g | Fat: 17.3g | Fiber: 10.2g

Ingredients

- One banana (cut in chunks)
- Half cup of blueberry yogurt
- One cup of kale (chopped)
- Half ripe avocado
- One-third cup of almond milk

Method:

1. Add blueberry, banana, avocado, and kale in a blender. Blend for making a smooth mixture.
2. Add the almond milk and blend again.
3. Divide the smoothie in glasses and serve.

Celery Pineapple Smoothie

Total Prep & Cooking Time: Ten minutes

Yields: Two servings

Nutrition Facts: Calories: 112 | Protein: 2.3g | Carbs: 3.6g | Fat: 1.2g | Fiber: 3.9g

Ingredients

- Three celery stalks (chopped)
- One cup of cubed pineapple
- One banana
- One pear
- Half cup of almond milk
- One tsp. of honey

Method:

1. Add celery stalks, pear, banana, and cubes of pineapple in a food processor. Blend until frothy and smooth.
2. Add honey and almond milk. Blend for two minutes.
3. Pour the smoothie in serving glasses and enjoy!

Cucumber Mango and Lime Smoothie

Total Prep & Cooking Time: Ten minutes

Yields: Two servings

Nutrition Facts: Calories: 165 | Protein: 2.2g | Carbs: 32.5g | Fat: 4.2g | Fiber: 3.7g

Ingredients

- One cup of ripe mango (frozen, cubed)
- Six cubes of ice
- Half cup of baby spinach leaves
- Two leaves of mint
- Two tsps. of lime juice
- Half cucumber (chopped)
- Three-fourth cup of coconut milk
- One-eighth tsp. of cayenne pepper

Method:

1. Add mango cubes, spinach leaves, and cucumber in a high power blender. Blend until frothy and smooth.
2. Add mint leaves, lime juice, coconut milk, cayenne pepper, and ice cubes. Process the ingredients until smooth.
3. Pour the smoothie in glasses and serve.

Kale, Melon, and Broccoli Smoothie

Total Prep & Cooking Time: Ten minutes

Yields: One serving

Nutrition Facts: Calories: 96.3 | Protein: 2.3g | Carbs: 24.3g | Fat: 1.2g | Fiber: 2.6g

Ingredients

- Eight ounces of honeydew melon
- One handful of kale
- Two ounces of broccoli florets
- One cup of coconut water
- Two sprigs of mint
- Two dates
- Half cup of lime juice
- Eight cubes of ice

Method:

1. Add kale, melon, and broccoli in a food processor. Whizz the ingredients for blending.
2. Add mint leaves and coconut water. Blend again.
3. Add lime juice, dates, and ice cubes. Blend the ingredients until smooth and creamy.
4. Pour the smoothie in a smoothie glass. Enjoy!

Kiwi Spinach Smoothie

Total Prep & Cooking Time: Ten minutes

Yields: Two servings

Nutrition Facts: Calories: 102 | Protein: 3.6g | Carbs: 21.3g | Fat: 2.2g | Fiber: 3.1g

Ingredients

- One kiwi (cut in chunks)
- One banana (cut in chunks)
- One cup of spinach leaves
- Three-fourth cup of almond milk
- One tbsp. of chia seeds
- Four cubes of ice

Method:

1. Add banana, kiwi, and spinach leaves in a blender. Blend the ingredients until smooth.
2. Add chia seeds, ice cubes, and almond milk. Blend again for one minute.
3. Pour the smoothie in serving glasses and serve.

Avocado Smoothie

Total Prep & Cooking Time: Ten minutes

Yields: Two servings

Nutrition Facts: Calories: 345 | Protein: 9.1g | Carbs: 47.8g | Fat: 16.9g | Fiber: 6.7g

Ingredients

- One ripe avocado (halved, pitted)
- One cup of milk
- Half cup of vanilla yogurt
- Eight cubes of ice
- Three tbsps. of honey

Method:

1. Add avocado, vanilla yogurt, and milk in a blender. Blend the ingredients until frothy and smooth.
2. Add honey and ice cubes. Blend the ingredients for making a smooth mixture.
3. Serve immediately.

PART II

Chapter 1: Meal Planning 101

Sticking to a diet is something that is not the easiest in the world. When it comes down to it, we struggle to change up our diets on a whim. It might be that for the first few days, you are able to stick to it and make sure that you are only eating those foods that are better for you, but over time, you will get to a point where you feel the pressure to cave in. You might realize that sticking to your diet is difficult and think that stopping for a burger on your way home won't be too bad. You might think that figuring out lunch or dinner is too much of a hassle, or you realize that the foods that you have bought forgot a key ingredient that you needed for dinner.

The good news is, you have an easy fix. When you are able to figure out what you are making for yourself for your meals well in advance, you stop having to worry so much about the foods that you eat, what you do with them, and what you are going to reach for when it's time to eat. You will be able to change up what you are doing so that you can be certain that the meals that you are enjoying are good for you, and you won't have to worry so much about the stress that goes into it. Let's take a look at what you need to do to get started with meal planning so that you can begin to do so without having to think too much about it.

Make a Menu

First, before you do anything, make sure that you make a menu! This should be something that you do on your own, or you should sit down with your family to ask them what they prefer. If you can do this, you will be able to ensure that you've got a clear-cut plan. When you have a menu a week in advance, you save yourself time and money because you know that all of your meals will use ingredients that are similar, and you won't have to spend forever thinking about what you should make at any point in time.

Plan around Ads

When you do your menu, make it a point to glance through the weekly ads as well. Typically, you will find that there are plenty of deals that you can make use of that will save you money.

Go Meatless Once Per Week

A great thing to do that is highly recommended on the Mediterranean Diet is to have a day each week where you go meatless for dinner. By doing so, you will realize that you can actually cut costs and enjoy the foods more at the same time. It is a great way to get that additional fruit and veggie content into your day, and there are plenty of healthy options that are out there for you. You just have to commit to doing so. In the meal plans that you'll see below, you will notice that there will be a meatless day on Day 2 every week.

Use Ingredients That You Already Have On Hand

Make it a point to use ingredients that you already have on hand whenever possible. Alternatively, make sure that all of the meals that you eat during the week use very similar ingredients. When you do this, you know that you're avoiding causing any waste or losing ingredients along the way, meaning that you can save money. The good news is, on the Mediterranean diet, there are plenty of delicious meals that enjoy very similar ingredients that you can eat.

Avoid Recipes that Call for a Special Ingredient

If you're trying to avoid waste, it is a good idea for you to avoid any ingredients in meals that are not going to carry over to other meals during your weekly plan. By avoiding doing so, you can usually save yourself that money for that one ingredient that would be wasted. Alternatively, if you find that you really want that dish, try seeing if you can freeze some of it for later. When you do that, you can usually ensure that your special ingredient at least didn't go to waste.

Use Seasonal Foods

Fruits and veggies are usually cheaper when you buy them in season, and even better, when you do so, you will be enjoying a basic factor of the Mediterranean diet just by virtue of enjoying the foods when they are fresh. Fresher foods are usually tastier, and they also tend to carry more vitamins and minerals because they have not had the chance to degrade over time.

Make Use of Leftovers and Extra Portions

One of the greatest things that you can do when it comes to meal planning is to make use of your leftovers and make-ahead meals. When you do this regularly, making larger portions than you need, you can then use the extras as lunches and dinners all week long, meaning that you won't have to be constantly worrying about the food that you eat for lunch. We will use some of these in the meal plans that you will see as well.

Eat What You Enjoy

Finally, the last thing to remember with your meal plan is that you ought to be enjoying the foods that are on it at all times. When you ensure that the foods that you have on your plate are those that you actually enjoy, sticking to your meal plan doesn't become such a chore, and that means that you will be able to do better as well with your own diet. Your meal plan should be loaded up with foods that you are actually excited about enjoying. Meal planning and dieting should not be a drag—you should love every moment of it!

Chapter 2: 1 Month Meal Plan

This meal plan is designed to be used for one month to help you simplify making sure that you have delicious meals to eat without having to think. These meals are fantastic options if you don't know where to start but want to enjoy your Mediterranean diet without much hassle. For each of the five weeks included, you will get one breakfast recipe, one lunch recipe, one dinner recipe, and one snack recipe to make meal planning a breeze. So, give these recipes a try! Many of them are so delicious, you'll want to enjoy them over and over again!

Week 1: Success is no accident—you have to reach for it

Mediterranean Breakfast Sandwich

Serves: 4

Time: 20 minutes

Ingredients:

- Baby spinach (2 c.)
- Eggs (4)

- Fresh rosemary (1 Tbsp.)
- Low-fat feta cheese (4 Tbsp.)
- Multigrain sandwich thins (4)
- Olive oil (4 tsp.)
- Salt and pepper according to preference
- Tomato (1, cut into 8 slices)

Instructions:

1. Preheat your oven. This recipe works best at 375° F. Cut the sandwich things in half and brush the insides with half of your olive oil. Place the things on a baking sheet and toast for about five minutes or until the edges are lightly browned and crispy.
2. In a large skillet, heat the rest of your olive oil and the rosemary. Use medium-high heat. Crack your eggs into the skillet one at a time. Cook until the whites have set while keeping the yolks runny. Break the yolks and flip the eggs until done.
3. Serve by placing spinach in between two sandwich thins, along with two tomato slices, an egg, and a tablespoon of feta cheese.

Greek Chicken Bowls

Serves: 4

Time: 20 minutes

Ingredients:

- Arugula (4 c.)
- Chicken breast tenders (1 lb.)

- Cucumber (1, diced)
- Curry powder (1 Tbsp.)
- Dried basil (1 tsp.)
- Garlic powder (1 tsp.)
- Kalamata olives (2 Tbsp.)
- Olive oil (1 Tbsp.)
- Pistachios (0.25 c., chopped)
- Red onion (half, sliced)
- Sunflower seeds (0.25 c.)
- Tzatziki sauce (1 c.)

Instructions:

1. In a bowl, mix in the chicken tenders, curry powder, dried basil, and garlic powder. Make sure to coat the chicken evenly.
2. Heat one tablespoon of olive oil over medium-high. Add the chicken and cook for about four minutes on each side. Remove from the pan and set aside to cool.
3. Place one cup of arugula into four bowls. Toss in the diced cucumber, onion, and kalamata olives.
4. Chop the chicken and distribute evenly between the four bowls.
5. Top with tzatziki sauce, pistachio seeds, and sunflower seeds.

Ratatouille

Serves: 8

Time: 1 hour 30 minutes

Ingredients:

- Crushed tomatoes (1 28 oz. can)
- Eggplants (2)
- Fresh basil (4 Tbsp., chopped)
- Fresh parsley (2 Tbsp., chopped)
- Fresh thyme (2 tsp.)
- Garlic cloves (4, minced and 1 tsp, minced)
- Olive oil (6 Tbsp.)
- Onion (1, diced)
- Red bell pepper (1, diced)
- Roma tomatoes (6)
- Salt and pepper to personal preference
- Yellow bell pepper (1, diced)
- Yellow squashes (2)
- Zucchinis (2)

Instructions:

1. Get your oven ready. This recipe works best at 375° F.
2. Slice the tomatoes, eggplant, squash, and zucchini into thin rounds and set them to the side.

3. Heat up two tablespoons of olive oil in an oven safe pan using medium-high heat. Sauté your onions, four cloves of garlic, and bell peppers for about ten minutes or when soft. Add in your pepper and salt along with the full can of crushed tomatoes. Add in two tablespoons of basil. Stir thoroughly.

4. Take the vegetable slices from earlier and arrange them on top of the sauce in a pattern of your choosing. For example, a slice of eggplant, followed by a slice of tomato, squash, and zucchini, then repeating. Start from the outside and work inward to the center of your pan. Sprinkle salt and pepper overtop the veggies.

5. In a bowl, toss in the remaining basil and garlic, thyme, parsley, salt, pepper, and the rest of the olive oil. Mix it all together, and spoon over the veggies.

6. Cover your pan and bake for 40 minutes. Uncover and then continue baking for another 20 minutes.

Snack Platter

Serves: 6

Time:

Ingredients:

Rosemary Almonds

- Butter (1 Tbsp.)

- Dried rosemary (2 tsp.)
- Salt (pinch)
- Whole almonds (2 c.)

Hummus

- Chickpeas (1 15 oz. can, drained and rinsed)
- Garlic clove (1, peeled)
- Lemon (half, juiced)
- Olive oil (2 Tbsp.)
- Salt and pepper according to personal preference
- Tahini (2 Tbsp.)
- Water (2 Tbsp.)

Other sides

- Bell pepper (1, sliced)
- Cucumber (1, sliced)
- Feta cheese (4 oz, cubed)
- Kalamata olives (handful, drained)
- Pepperoncini peppers (6, drained)
- Pitas (6, sliced into wedges)
- Small fresh mozzarella balls (18)
- Soppressata (6 oz.)
- Sweet cherry peppers (18)

Instructions:

1. To get started, make your rosemary almonds. Take a large skillet and place it on a burner set to medium heat. Start melting the butter in, then toss in the almonds, rosemary and a bit of salt. Toss the nuts on occasion to ensure even coating.
2. Cook the almonds for roughly ten minutes, getting them nicely toasted. Set the almonds off to the side to let them cool.
3. Now you'll set out to make the hummus. Take a blender or food processor and toss in the hummus ingredients. Blend until you get a nice, smooth paste. If you find that your paste is too thick, try blending in a bit of water until you get the desired consistency. Once you have the right consistency, taste for seasoning and adjust as necessary.
4. Pour and scrape the hummus into a bowl and drizzle in a bit of olive oil. Set it off to the side to get the rest of the platter going.
5. Grab the sweet cherry peppers and stuff them with the little balls of mozzarella. Arrange a platter in any pattern you like. If serving for a party or family, try keeping each snack in its own little segment to keep things looking neat.

Week 2: Self-belief and effort will take you to what you want to achieve

Breakfast Quesadilla

Serves: 1

Time: 10 minutes

Ingredients:

- Basil (handful)
- Eggs (2)
- Flour tortilla (1)

- Green pesto (1 tsp.)
- Mozzarella (0.25 c.)
- Salt and pepper according to personal preference
- Tomato (half, sliced)

Instructions:

1. Scramble your eggs until just a little runny. Remember, you will be cooking them further inside the quesadilla. Season with salt and pepper.
2. Take the eggs and spread over half of the tortilla.
3. Add basil, pesto, mozzarella cheese, and the slices of tomato.
4. Fold your tortilla and toast on an oiled pan. Toast until both sides are golden brown.

Greek Orzo Salad

Serves: 6

Time: 25 minutes

Ingredients:

- Canned chickpeas (1 c., drained and rinsed)
- Dijon mustard (0.5 tsp)
- Dill (0.33 c., chopped)
- Dried oregano (1 tsp)
- English cucumber (half, diced)
- Feta cheese crumbles (0.5 c.)
- Kalamata olives (0.33 c., halved)
- Lemon (half, juice and zest)
- Mint (0.33 c., chopped)
- Olive oil (3 Tbsp.)
- Orzo pasta (1.25 c. when dry)
- Roasted red pepper (half, diced)
- Salt and pepper to taste
- Shallot (0.25 c., minced)
- White wine vinegar (2 Tbsp.)

Instructions:

1. Prepare the orzo according to the packaging details. Once the orzo is al dente, drain it and rinse until it drops to room temperature.
2. In a bowl, toss all the ingredients together until thoroughly incorporated.

One Pot Mediterranean Chicken

Serves: 4

Time: 1 hour

Ingredients:

- Chicken broth (3 c.)
- Chicken thighs (3, bone in, skin on)

- Chickpeas (1 15 oz can, drained and rinsed)
- Dried oregano (0.5 tsp.)
- Fresh parsley (2 Tbsp., chopped)
- Garlic cloves (2, minced)
- Kalamata olives (0.75 c., halved)
- Olive oil (2 tsp.)
- Onion (1, finely diced)
- Orzo pasta (8 ounces uncooked)
- Roasted peppers (0.5 c., chopped)
- Salt and pepper according to personal preference

Instructions:

1. Prepare your oven at 375°. Heat your olive oil in a large skillet over medium-high heat.
2. Season the chicken with salt and pepper on both sides. Toss the chicken into the skillet and cook for five minutes on each side, or until golden in color. Remove the chicken.
3. Take the skillet and drain most of the rendered fat, leaving about a teaspoon. Add the onion and cook for five minutes. Toss in the garlic and cook for an additional minute.
4. Now you will want to add the orzo, roasted peppers, oregano, chickpeas, and olives into the pan. Add in salt and pepper.
5. Place the thighs on top of the orzo and pour in the chicken broth.
6. Bring to a boil, then cover and place in the oven. Bake for 35 minutes or until chicken has cooked through. Top with parsley and serve.

Mediterranean Nachos

Serves: 6

Time: 10 minutes

Ingredients:

- Canned artichoke hearts (1 c., rinsed, drained, and dried)
- Canned garbanzo beans (0.75 c., rinsed, drained, and dried)
- Feta cheese (0.5 c., crumbled)
- Fresh cilantro (2 Tbsp., chopped)
- Pine nuts (2.5 Tbsp.)
- Roasted red peppers (0.5 c., dried)
- Sabra Hummus (half of their 10 oz. container)
- Tomatoes (0.5 c., chopped)
- Tortilla chips (roughly half a bag)

Instructions:

1. Get your oven ready by setting it to 375°F. In a baking pan, layer the tortilla chips, and spread hummus over them evenly. Top with garbanzo beans, red peppers, artichoke hearts, feta cheese, and pine nuts.
2. Bake for about five minutes or until warmed through. Remove the baking pan and top the nachos with fresh cilantro and tomatoes. Serve and enjoy.

Week 3: The harder you work, the greater the success

Breakfast Tostadas

Serves: 4

Time: 15 minutes

Ingredients:

- Beaten eggs (8)
- Cucumber (0.5 c., seeded and chopped)
- Feta (0.25 c., crumbled)
- Garlic powder (0.5 tsp)
- Green onions (0.5 c., chopped)
- Oregano (0.5 tsp)
- Red Pepper (0.5 c., diced)
- Roasted red pepper hummus (0.5 c.)
- Skim milk (0.5 c.)
- Tomatoes (0.5 c., diced)
- Tostadas (4)

Instructions:

1. In a large skillet, cook the red pepper for two minutes on medium heat until softened. Toss in the eggs, garlic powder, milk, oregano, and green onions. Stir constantly until the egg whites have set.
2. Top the tostadas with hummus, egg mixture, cucumber, feta, and tomatoes.

Roasted Vegetable Bowl

Serves: 2

Time: 45 minutes

Ingredients:

- Crushed red pepper flakes (a pinch)
- Fresh parsley (1 Tbsp., chopped)
- Kalamata olives (0.25 c.)
- Kale (1 c., ribboned)
- Lemon juice (1 Tbsp.)
- Marinated artichoke hearts (0.25 c., drained and chopped)
- Nutritional yeast (1 Tbsp.)
- Olive oil (1 Tbsp., then enough to drizzle)
- Salt and pepper to taste

- Spaghetti squash (half, seeds removed)
- Sun-dried tomatoes (2 Tbsp., chopped)
- Walnuts (0.25 c., chopped)

Instructions:

1. Get your oven ready by setting it to 400° F. Take a baking sheet and blanket it with parchment paper.
2. Take the squash half and place it on the parchment paper. Drizzle olive oil over the side that is cut, and season with salt and pepper. Turn it over so it is facing cut side down and bake for 40 minutes. It is ready when it is soft.
3. Remove the squash shell, and season with a bit more salt and pepper.
4. Stack the kale, artichoke hearts, walnuts, sun-dried tomatoes, and kalamata olives on the squash.
5. Squeeze the lemon juice over and drizzle olive oil. Finish with chopped parsley and a bit of crushed red pepper flakes.

Mediterranean Chicken

Serves: 4

Time: 40 minutes

Ingredients:

- Chicken breasts (1 lb., boneless, skinless)
- Chives (2 Tbsp., chopped)
- Feta cheese (0.25 c., crumbled)
- Garlic (1 tsp., minced)
- Italian seasoning (1 tsp.)
- Lemon juice (2 Tbsp.)
- Olive oil (2 Tbsp., and 1 Tbsp.)
- Salt and pepper according to personal preference
- Tomatoes (1 c., diced)

Instructions:

1. Pour in two tablespoons of olive oil, the lemon juice, salt, pepper, garlic, and Italian seasoning in a resealable plastic bag. Add in the chicken, seal and shake to coat the chicken.
2. Allow the chicken to marinate for at least 30 minutes in the refrigerator.
3. Heat the rest of the olive oil in a pan over medium heat.
4. Place the chicken on the pan and cook for five minutes on each side, or until cooked through.
5. In a bowl, mix the tomatoes, chives, and feta cheese. Season with salt and pepper.
6. When serving, spoon the tomato mixture on top of the chicken.

Baked Phyllo Chips

Serves: 2

Time: 10 minutes

Ingredients:

- Grated cheese (your choice)
- Olive oil (enough to brush with)
- Phyllo sheets (4)
- Salt and pepper according to personal preference

Instructions:

1. Get your oven ready by setting it to 350° F. Brush olive oil over a phyllo sheet generously. Sprinkle grated cheese and your seasoning on top.
2. Grab a second sheet of your phyllo and place it on top of the first one. Again, brush with olive oil and sprinkle cheese and seasoning on top.
3. Repeat this process with the remaining sheets of phyllo. Top the stack with cheese and seasoning.
4. Once complete, cut the stack of phyllo into bite-sized rectangles. A pizza cutter may be helpful here.
5. Grab a baking sheet and blanket it with some parchment paper. Take your phyllo rectangles and place them on the parchment paper.
6. Bake in the oven for about seven minutes or until they reach a golden color.
7. Remove them from the oven and allow them to cool before serving.

Week 4: You don't need perfection—you need effort

Mini Omelets

Serves: 8

Time: 40 minutes

Ingredients:

- Cheddar cheese (0.25 c., shredded)
- Eggs (8)
- Half and half (0.5 c.)
- Olive oil (2 tsps.)
- Salt and pepper according to personal preference
- Spinach (1 c., chopped)

Instructions:

1. Get your oven ready by setting it to 350° F. Prepare a muffin pan or ramekins by greasing them with olive oil.
2. In a bowl, beat the eggs and dairy until you have a fluffy consistency.
3. Stir in the cheese and your seasonings. Pour in the spinach and continue beating the eggs.
4. Pour the egg mixture into your ramekins or muffin pan.
5. Bake the omelets until they have set, which should be roughly 25 minutes. Remove them from the oven and allow them to cool before serving.

Basil Shrimp Salad

Serves: 2

Time: 40 minutes

Ingredients:

- Dried basil (1 tsp.)
- Lemon juice (1 Tbsp.)
- Olive oil (1 tsp.)
- Romaine lettuce (2 c.)
- Shrimp (12 medium or 8 large)
- White wine vinegar (0.25 c.)

Instructions:

1. Whisk together the white wine vinegar, olive oil, lemon juice, and basil. Stick your shrimp in the marinade for half an hour.
2. Take the marinade and shrimp and cook in a skillet over medium heat until cooked through.
3. Allow the shrimp to cool along with the juice and pour into a bowl. Toss in the romaine lettuce and mix well to get the flavor thoroughly infused in the salad. Serve.

Mediterranean Flounder

Serves: 4

Time: 40 minutes

Ingredients:

- Capers (0.25 c.)
- Diced tomatoes (1 can)
- Flounder fillets (1 lb.)
- Fresh basil (12 leaves, chopped)
- Fresh parmesan cheese (3 Tbsp., grated)
- Garlic cloves (2, chopped)
- Italian seasoning (a pinch)
- Kalamata olives (0.5 c., pitted and chopped)
- Lemon juice (1 tsp.)

- Red onion (half, chopped)
- White wine (0.25 c.)

Instructions:

1. Set your oven to 425° F. Take a skillet and pour in enough olive oil to sauté the onion until soft. Cook on medium-high heat.
2. Toss in the garlic, Italian seasoning, and tomatoes. Cook for an additional five minutes.
3. Pour in the wine, capers, olives, lemon juice, and only half of the basil you chopped.
4. Reduce the heat to low and stir in the parmesan cheese. Simmer for ten minutes or until the sauce has thickened.
5. Place the flounder fillets in a baking pan and pour the sauce over top. Sprinkle the remaining basil on top and bake for 12 minutes.

Nutty Energy Bites

Serves: 10

Time: 10 minutes

Ingredients:

- Dried dates (1 c., pitted)
- Almonds (0.5 c.)

- Pine nuts (0.25 c.)
- Flaxseeds (1 Tbsp., milled) Porridge oats (2 Tbsp.)
- Pistachios (0.25 c., coarsely ground)

Instructions:

1. Take the dates, pine nuts, milled flaxseeds, almonds, and porridge oats and pour them into a food processor or blender. Mix until thoroughly incorporated.
2. Using a tablespoon, scoop the mixture and roll it between your hands until you have a small, bite-sized ball. Do this until you have used the entirety of the dough. This recipe should be enough for about ten.
3. On a plate, sprinkle your ground pistachios. Take the energy balls and roll them on the pistachio grounds, making sure to coat them evenly. Serve or store in the refrigerator.

Week 5: Transformation Happens One Day at a Time

Mediterranean Breakfast Bowl

Serves: 1

Time: 25 minutes

Ingredients:

- Artichoke hearts (0.25 c., chopped)
- Baby arugula (2 c.)
- Capers (1 Tbsp.)
- Egg (1)
- Feta (2 Tbsp., crumbled)
- Garlic (0.25 tsp)
- Kalamata olives (5, chopped)
- Lemon thyme (1 Tbsp., chopped)
- Olive oil (0.5 Tbsp.)
- Pepper (0.25 tsp)
- Sun-dried tomatoes (2 Tbsp., chopped)
- Sweet potato (1 c., cubed)

Instructions:

1. Take your olive oil and, when hot, pan fry your sweet potatoes for 5-10 minutes until they have softened. Then, sprinkle on the seasonings.
2. Place arugula into a bowl, then top with potatoes, then everything but the egg.
3. Prepare the egg to your liking and serve.

Chicken Shawarma Pita Pockets

Serves: 6

Time: 40 minutes

Ingredients:

- Cayenne (0.5 tsp)
- Chicken thighs (8, boneless, skinless, bite-sized pieces)
- Cloves (0.5 tsp, ground)
- Garlic powder (0.75 Tbsp.)
- Ground cumin (0.75 Tbsp.)
- Lemon juice (1 lemon)
- Olive oil (0.33 c.)
- Onion (1, sliced thinly)
- Paprika (0.75 Tbsp.)
- Salt
- Turmeric powder (0.75 Tbsp.)

To serve:

- Pita pockets (6)
- Tzatziki sauce
- Arugula
- Diced tomatoes
- Diced onions
- Sliced Kalamata olives

Instructions:

1. Combine all spices. Then, place all chicken, already diced, into the bowl. Coat well, then toss in onions, lemon juice, and oil. Mix well and let marinade for at least 3 hours, or overnight.
2. Preheat the oven to 425 F. Allow chicken to sit at room temperature a few minutes. Then, spread it on an oiled sheet pan. Roast for 30 minutes.
3. To serve, fill up a pita pocket with tzatziki, chicken, arugula, and any toppings you prefer. Enjoy.

Turkey Mediterranean Casserole

Serves: 6

Time: 35 minutes

Ingredients:

- Fusilli pasta (0.5 lbs.)
- Turkey (1.5 c., chopped)
- Sun dried tomatoes (2 Tbsp., drained)
- Canned artichokes (7 oz., drained)
- Kalamata olives (3.5 oz., drained and chopped)
- Parsley (0.5 Tbsp., chopped and fresh)
- Basil (1 T, fresh)
- Salt and pepper to taste
- Marinara sauce (1 c.)

- Black chopped olives (2 oz., drained)
- Mozzarella cheese (1.5 c., shredded)

Instructions:

1. Warm your oven to 350 F. Prepare your pasta according to the directions, drain, and place into a bowl. Prepare your basil, parsley, olives, tomatoes, artichokes, and other ingredients.
2. Mix together the pasta with the turkey, tomatoes, olives, artichokes, herbs, seasoning, and marinara sauce. Give it a good mix to incorporate all of the ingredients evenly.
3. Take a 9x13 oven-safe dish and layer in the first half of your pasta mixture. Then, sprinkle on half of your mozzarella cheese. Top with the rest of the pasta, then sprinkle on the chopped black olives as well. Spread the rest of the shredded cheese on top, then bake it for 20-25 minutes. It is done when the cheese is all bubbly and the casserole is hot.

Heirloom Tomato and Cucumber Toast

Serves: 2

Time: 5 minutes

Ingredients:

- Heirloom tomato (1, diced)
- Persian cucumber (1, diced)
- Extra virgin olive oil (1 tsp)
- Oregano (a pinch, dried)
- Kosher salt and pepper
- Whipped cream cheese (2 tsp)
- Whole grain bread (2 pieces)
- Balsamic glaze (1 tsp)

Instructions:

4. Combine the tomato, cucumber, oil, and all seasonings together.
5. Spread cheese across bread, then top with mixture, followed by balsamic glaze.

Chapter 3: Maintaining Your Diet

Sticking to a diet can be tough. You could see that other people are having some great food and wish that you could enjoy it too. You might realize that you miss the foods that you used to eat and feel like it's a drag to not be able to enjoy them. When you are able to enjoy the foods that you are eating, sticking to your diet is far easier. However, that doesn't mean that you won't miss those old foods sometimes. Thankfully, the Mediterranean diet is not a very restrictive one—you are able to enjoy foods in moderation that would otherwise not be allowed, and because of that, you can take the slice of cake at the work party, or you can choose to pick up a coffee for yourself every now and then. When you do this, you're not doing anything wrong, so long as you enjoy food in moderation.

Within this chapter, we are going to take a look at several tips that you can use that will help you with maintaining your diet so that you will be able to stick to it, even when you feel like things are getting difficult. Think of this as your guide to avoiding giving in entirely—this will help you to do the best thing for yourself so that you can know that you are healthy. Now, let's get started.

Find Your Motivation

First, if you want to keep yourself on your diet, one of the best things that you can do is make sure that you find and stick to your motivation. Make sure that you know what it is in life that is motivating you. Are you losing weight because a doctor told you to? Fair enough—but how do you make that personal and about yourself? Maybe instead of looking at it as a purely health-related choice, look at it as something that you are doing because of yourself. Maybe you are eating better so that you are able to watch your children graduate or so that you can run after them at the park and stay healthy, even when it is hard to do so.

Remind Yourself Why You are Eating Healthily

When you find that you are struggling to eat healthily, remind yourself of why you are doing it in the first place. When you do this enough, you will begin to resist the urges easier than ever. Make it a point to tell yourself not to eat something a certain way. Take the time to remind yourself that you don't need to order that greasy pizza—you are eating better foods because you want to be there for your children or grandchildren.

Reminding yourself of your motivation is a great way to overcome those cravings that you may have at any point in time. The cravings that you have are usually strong and compelling, but if you learn to overcome them, you realize that they weren't actually as powerful as you thought they were. Defeat the cravings. Learn to tell yourself that they are not actually able to control you. Tell yourself that you can do better with yourself.

Eat Slowly

Now, on the Mediterranean diet, you should already be eating your meals with other people anyway. You should be taking the time to enjoy those meals while talking to other people and ensuring that you get that connection with them, and in doing so, you realize that you are able to do better. You realize that you are able to keep yourself under control longer, and that is a great way to defend and protect yourself from overeating.

When you eat slowly, you can get the same effect. Eating slowly means that you will have longer for your brain to realize that you should be eating less. When you are able to trigger that sensation of satiety because you were eating slowly, you end up eating fewer calories by default, and that matters immensely.

Keep Yourself Accountable

Don't forget that, ultimately, your diet is something that you must control on your own. Keep yourself accountable by making sure that you show other people what you are doing. If you are trying to lose weight, let them know, and tell them how you plan to do so. When you do this, you are able to remind yourself that other people know what you are doing and why—this is a great way to foster that sense of accountability because you will feel like you have to actually follow through, or you will be embarrassed by having to admit fault. You could also make accountability to yourself as well. When you do this, you are able to remind yourself that your diet is your own. Using apps to track your food and caloric intake is just one way that you can do this.

Remember Your Moderation

While it can be difficult to face a diet where you feel like you can't actually enjoy the foods that you would like to eat, the truth is that on the Mediterranean diet, you are totally okay to eat those foods that you like or miss if you do so in moderation. There is nothing that is absolutely forbidden on the Mediterranean diet—there are just foods that you should be restricting regularly. However, that doesn't mean that you can't have a treat every now and then.

Remembering to live in moderation will help you from feeling like you have to cheat or give up as well. When you are able to enjoy your diet and still enjoy the times where you want to enjoy your treats, you realize that there is actually a happy medium between sticking to the diet and deciding to quit entirely.

Identify the Difference between Hunger and Craving

Another great way to help yourself stick to your diet is to recognize that there is a very real difference between actually being hungry and just craving something to eat. In general, cravings are felt in the mouth—when you feel like you are salivating or like you need to eat something, but it is entirely in your head and mouth, you know that you have a craving. When you are truly hungry, you feel an emptiness in your stomach—you are able to know because your abdomen is where the motivation is coming from.

Being able to tell when you have a craving and when you are genuinely hungry, you can usually avoid eating extra calories that you didn't actually need. This is major—if you don't want to overeat, you need to know when your body actually needs something and when it just wants something. And if you find that you just want something, that's okay too—just find a way to move on from it. If you want to indulge a bit here and there, there's no harm in that!

Stick to the Meal Plan

When it comes to sticking to a diet, one of the easiest and most straightforward ways to do so is to just stick to your meal plan that you set up. You have it there for a reason—it is there for you to fall back on, and the sooner that you are willing to accept that, recognizing that ultimately, you can stay on track when you don't have to think about things too much, the better you will do. You will be able to succeed on your diet because you will know that you have those tools in place to protect you—they will be lined up to ensure that your diet is able to provide you with everything that you need and they will also be there so that you can know that you are on the right track.

Drink Plenty of Water

Another key to keeping yourself on track with your diet is to make sure that you drink plenty of water throughout the day. Oftentimes, we mistake our thirst with hunger and eat instead. Of course, if you're thirsty, food isn't going to really fix your problem, and you will end up continuing to mix up the sensation as you try to move past it. The more you eat, the thirstier you will get until you realize that you're full but still feeling "hungry." By drinking plenty of water any time that you think that you might want to eat, you will be able to keep yourself hydrated, and in addition, you will prevent yourself from unintentionally eating too much.

Eat Several Times Per Day

One of the best ways to keep yourself on track with your diet is to make sure that you are regularly eating. By eating throughout the day, making sure that you keep yourself full, it is easier to keep yourself strong enough to resist giving in to cravings or anything else. When you do this regularly, you will discover that you can actually keep away much of your cravings so that you are more successful in managing your diet.

Eating several times per day often involves small meals and snacks if you prefer to do so. Some people don't like doing this, but if you find that you're one of those people who will do well on a diet when you are never actually hungry enough to get desperate enough to break it, you will probably be just fine.

Fill Up on Protein

Another great way to protect yourself from giving in and caving on your diet is to make sure that you fill up on protein. Whether it comes from an animal or plant source, make sure that every time you eat, you have some sort of tangible protein source. This is the best way to keep yourself on track because protein keeps you fuller for longer. When you eat something that's loaded up with protein, you don't feel the need to eat as much later on. The protein is usually very dense, and that means that you get to resist feeling hungry for longer than you thought that you would.

Some easy proteins come from nuts—but make sure that you are mindful that you do not end up overeating during this process—you might unintentionally end up eating too many without realizing it. While you should be eating proteins regularly, make sure that you are mindful of calorie content as well!

Keep Only Healthy Foods

A common mistake that people make while dieting is that they end up caving when they realize that their home is filled up with foods that they shouldn't be eating. Perhaps you are the only person in your home that is attempting to diet. In this case, you may end up running into a situation where you have all sorts of non-compliant foods on hand. You might have chips for your kids or snacks that your partner likes to eat on hand. You may feel like it is difficult for you to stay firm when you have that to consider, and that means that you end up stuck in temptation.

One of the best ways to prevent this is to either cut all of the unhealthy junk out of your home entirely or make sure that you keep the off-limits foods in specific places so that you don't have to look at it and see it tempting you every time that you go to get a snack for yourself. By trying to keep yourself limited to just healthy foods, you will be healthier, and you will make better decisions.

Eat Breakfast Daily

Finally, make sure that breakfast is non-negotiable. Make sure that you enjoy it every single day, even if you're busy. This is where those make-ahead meals can come in handy; by knowing that you have to keep to a meal plan and knowing that you already have the food on hand, you can keep yourself fed. Breakfast sets you up for success or failure—if you want to truly succeed on your diet, you must make sure that you are willing to eat those healthier foods as much as possible, and you must get started on the right foot. Enjoy those foods first thing every day. Eat so that you are not ravenous when you finally do decide that it is time to sit down and find something to eat. Even if you just have a smoothie or something quick to eat as you go, having breakfast will help you to persevere.

PART III

Chapter 1: Identifying the Mediterranean Diet

We know that certain diets are associated with better health—this is a simple fact of life. We've seen that entire groups of people live longer based on where they live, and to some degree, a good deal of that has to come from somewhere—it has to come from something like diet or environment. In this case, the diet of the people living in the Mediterranean has been found to be incredibly healthy for people—it has been shown that people who are able to enjoy this diet, who are able to eat fresh food by the sea and enjoy the benefits that it has, are able to be far healthier than those who don't have it. That is great for them—but what is their secret?

It turns out, it's all in the lifestyle. The Mediterranean lifestyle, food, and all, is incredibly healthy for you. Studies have shown that people living in Mediterranean countries such as Greece and Italy have been found to have far less risk of death from coronary disease. Their secret is in the diet. Their diet has been shown to reduce the risk of cardiovascular disease, meaning that it is incredibly healthy, beneficial, and something that the vast majority of people in the world could definitely benefit from.

The Mediterranean diet is recommended by doctors and the World Health Organization as being not only healthy but also sustainable, meaning that it is something that is highly recommended, even by the experts. If you've found that you've struggled with weight loss, heart disease, managing your blood pressure, or anything similar to those problems, then the Mediterranean diet is for you.

When you follow this diet, you are able to bring health back to your life and enjoy the foods while doing so. It's perfect if you want to be able to enjoy your diet without having to worry about the impacts that it will have on you.

Defining the Mediterranean Lifestyle

The Mediterranean diet is quite simple. It involves eating traditional foods based on one's location. Typically, in the Mediterranean, that is a diet that is rich in veggies, fruits, whole grains, beans, and features olive oil as the fat of choice. Typically, it involves elements beyond just eating as well. While it is important to have healthy food, it is equally important to recognize that the diet encompasses the lifestyle as well. In particular, you can expect to see a few other rules come into play.

In particular, the Mediterranean diet is unique in the sense that it encourages a glass of red wine every now and then. In fact, the diet is associated with moderate drinking, enjoying red wine several times per week, always responsibly, and in contexts that will be beneficial to the drinker. If you want to be able to enjoy the Mediterranean diet and you are pregnant, or against drinking, you can do that, too—but traditionally, the red wine is included and even encouraged in moderation thanks to the antioxidants within it.

Additionally, on the Mediterranean diet, it is common to share meals with friends and family. This is essential—eating is more than just filling the body, it is nurturing the mind and relationships as well. This also comes with the added benefit of also being able to slow down eating—when you are eating the foods on this diet, you will discover that ultimately, you eat less when you're busy having a riveting conversation with someone. The fact that you are slowed down with your eating means that you will fill up sooner and realize that you didn't have to actually eat the food that you did. This means that you eat less and are, therefore managing your portions better as a result.

Finally, the Mediterranean diet focuses on physical activity. Traditionally, you would have had to go out to get the foods that you would eat each day, and that would mean that you'd need to get up, fish, garden, farm, or otherwise prepare your food. Eating locally is still a major component of this diet, as is getting up and being active. You need at least 30 minutes of activity, moderate or mild, per day. Even just walking for half an hour is better than nothing!

The Rules of the Mediterranean Diet

To eat the Mediterranean way, there are a few key factors that can guide you. If you know what you are doing, you can eat well without having to sacrifice flavor for health, and that matters immensely. When you look at the Mediterranean diet closely, you see that there are several tips that will help you to recognize what you need to do to stick to your diet.

Eating fruits and veggies

First, make sure that the bulk of your calories come from fruits and vegetables. You should be eating between 7 and 10 servings of fresh fruits and vegetables every single day—meaning that the bulk of your calories will come from there. Try to stick to locally grown foods that are fresh and in-season—they will have the highest nutritional value.

Reach for the whole grains

Yes, pasta is a major part of the diet in the Mediterranean, and you don't have to give that up entirely—but make sure that any grains that you are enjoying are whole-wheat. This allows you to enjoy foods that are high in fiber and are able to be digested differently than when you use refined carbs instead. While the refined carbs may give you instantaneous energy, they are also not nearly as good for you as whole wheat.

Using healthy fats

When it comes to flavoring or cooking your foods, you need to reach for the healthy fats first. This means choosing out foods that are cooked with olive oil instead of butter or dipping food in olive oil instead of butter. Olive oil, despite being a fat, has not been found to lead to weight gain when used in moderation. It is an incredibly healthy substitute for butter that is loaded up with all sorts of beneficial, heart-healthy antioxidants that will help your cardiovascular system.

Aim for seafood

When it comes to protein, fish, especially fresh fish, is the best choice. Fish should be consumed at least twice per week, and it should be fresh rather than frozen whenever possible. In particular, it is commonly recommended that you reach for salmon or trout, or other fatty fish because the omega-3 fatty acids within them are incredibly healthy for you, and they will serve you well. Even better, if you grill your fish, you have little cleanup.

Reduce red meat

In addition to adding more seafood to your diet, you need to cut out the red meat. The red meats in your diet are no good for you—they have been linked to inflammation that can make it harder for your cardiovascular system.

Enjoy dairy in moderation

When you are on this diet, dairy is not out of the picture entirely. While you should avoid butter, for the most part, it is a good idea for you to enjoy some low-fat Greek yogurt on occasion and add in some cheese to your diet. It is a good thing for you to enjoy these foods to ensure that you have plenty of calcium to keep your body strong.

Spices, not salt

Perhaps one of the most profound differences between most other diets and the Mediterranean diet is the lack of salt. The Mediterranean diet reaches for herbs and spices before adding in salt, meaning that you will be consuming less of it over time. Even better, you will grow to love your new foods without needing salt.

Chapter 2: Savory Mediterranean Meals

Mediterranean Feta Mac and Cheese

Ingredients

- Egg (1, beaten)
- Feta cheese (8 oz., crumbles)
- Macaroni (0.5 lb., whole-wheat)
- Olive oil (3 Tbsp.)
- Salt and pepper to taste
- Sour cream (8 oz.)

Instructions

1. Cook pasta to instructions to create al dente pasta. Drain and place pasta into baking dish. Toss in feta and oil and mix well.
2. Combine your egg and sour cream with salt and pepper. Then mix well and toss over macaroni. Combine and bake at 350F for 30 minutes.

Chickpea Stew

Ingredients

- Bay leaf (1)
- Dry chickpeas (1 c., soaked overnight and peeled)
- Garlic (1 clove, cut in half)
- Lemon to serve

- Olive oil (0.25 c.)
- Onion (1, diced)
- Salt and pepper to taste

Instructions

1. Cover chickpeas in pot with just enough water to cover them and wait to boil. Then rinse and set into clean pot. Toss in all other ingredients but the lemon with just enough water to cover nearly one inch above the beans. Simmer for 2-3 hours and serve with lemons.

Savory Mediterranean Breakfast Muffins

Ingredients

Dry ingredients

- Baking powder (1.5 tsp)
- Baking soda (o.5 tsp)
- Flour (2 c.)
- Salt (0.5 tsp)

Wet ingredients

- Egg (1 large)
- Garlic (1 clove, minced)
- Milk (1 c.)
- Sour cream (0.25 c.)
- Vegetable oil (0.25 c.)

Fillings

- Cheddar cheese (2 c., shredded)
- Feta (2.5 oz., crumbled)
- Green olives (diced, 0.5 c.)
- Green onions (0.5 c., chopped)
- Roasted red peppers (0.5 c., chopped)
- Sun dried tomatoes (diced, 0.5 c.)

Instructions

1. Combine dry ingredients in a bowl. Mix wet ingredients in separate bowl. Combine the two together and mix.
2. Toss in fillings in as few stirs as possible.
3. Place in greased or lined muffin pan, dividing to all 12 recesses.
4. Bake for 25 minutes until golden-brown and crusty at 350F.
5. Cool for 10 minutes and serve warm.

Mediterranean Breakfast Bake

Ingredients

- Artichoke hearts (14-oz. can, drained)
- Bread (6 slices whole-wheat, chopped)
- Eggs (8)
- Feta cheese (0.5 c.)
- Italian sausage (turkey or chicken—1 lb., casings removed)
- Milk (1 c.)
- Olive oil (2 Tbsp., divided)

- Onion (1, chopped)
- Spinach (5 oz.)
- Sun dried tomato (1 c., chopped)

Instructions

1. Warm 1 Tbsp. of your olive oil on moderately high heat. Cook sausage for 8 minutes until it has browned, breaking it up as it cooks. Place it in a dish when it is done.
2. Toss in additional oil, then cook onion until soft, roughly 5 minutes. Toss in spinach until wilting (1 minute).
3. Combine eggs and mix in milk, bread, tomatoes, cheese, artichokes, sausage, and finally, the spinach mix.
4. Place everything in a 2.5 quart baking dish. Let sit for an hour in fridge, or leave overnight.
5. Let casserole sit for 30 minutes after removing from fridge. Then, bake for 45 minutes at 350F until brown. Let rest 10 minutes, then serve.

Mediterranean Pastry Pinwheels

Ingredients

- Cream cheese (8-ounce package, softened)
- Pesto (0.25 c.)
- Provolone cheese (0.75 c.)
- Sun-dried tomatoes (0.5 c., chopped)
- Ripe olives (0.5 c., chopped)

Instructions

1. Unroll pastry and trim it up to create 10-inch square.

2. Mix together your cream cheese and pesto until well-combined. Then, mix in other ingredients until combined. Place mixture in even layer across pastry, up to 0.5-inch of edges. Roll and freeze for 30 minutes.

3. Cut whole roll into 16 pieces.

4. Bake at 400F until golden, roughly 15 minutes. Serve.

Chapter 3: Sweet Treats on the Mediterranean Diet

Greek Yogurt Parfait

Ingredients

- Almond butter (2 Tbsp.)
- Fresh fruit (1 Tbsp.)
- Greek Yogurt (1 c.)

Instructions

1. Mix together yogurt and 1 Tbsp. of almond butter and put in a bowl. Top with fruit.
2. Warm remaining butter in microwave for 10 minutes, then drizzle atop yogurt. Serve. You can add different toppings to change up the flavor as well.

Overnight Oats

Ingredients

- Chia seeds (1 Tbsp.)
- Greek yogurt (0.25 c.)
- Honey (1 Tbsp.)
- Milk of choice (0.5 c.)
- Old fashioned whole oats (0.5 c.)
- Vanilla extract (0.25 tsp)

Instructions

1. Mix all ingredients into a glass container and leave in fridge for at least 2 hours but preferably overnight. Serve with berries of choice or other desired toppings.

Apple Whipped Yogurt

Ingredients

- Greek yogurt (1 c.)
- Heavy cream (0.5 c.)
- Honey (1 Tbsp.)
- Unsalted butter (2 Tbsp.)
- Apples (2, cored and chopped into small bits)
- Sugar (2 Tbsp.)
- Cinnamon (1/8 tsp)
- Walnut halves (0.25 c., chopped)

Instructions

1. Using a hand mixer, mix together yogurt, honey, and honey until it creates peaks.
2. Heat up your butter in a skillet over a moderate temperature. Cook apples and 1 Tbsp. sugar in pan. Stir and cook for 6-8 minutes until soft. Then, top with the rest of sugar and cinnamon, stirring and cooking an additional 3 minutes. Take it off of the burner and let it rest for 5 minutes.
3. Serve with whipped yogurt in bowl topped with apple, then sprinkle on walnuts.

Chapter 4: Gourmet Meals on the Mediterranean Diet

Garlic-Roasted Salmon and Brussels Sprouts

Ingredients

- Brussels sprouts (6 c., trimmed and halved)
- Chardonnay (0.75 c.)
- Garlic cloves (14 large)
- Olive oil (0.25 c.)
- Oregano (2 Tbsp., fresh)
- Pepper (0.75 tsp)
- Salmon fillet (2 lbs., skin-off—cut in 6 pieces)
- Salt (1 tsp)
- Lemon wedges to serve

Instructions

1. Take two cloves of garlic and mince, combining them with oil, 1 Tbsp. of oregano, half of the salt and 1/3 of the pepper. Cut remaining cloves of garlic in halves and toss them with the sprouts. Take 3 Tbsp. of your garlic oil and toss it with the sprouts in roasting pan. Roast for 15 minutes at 450F.
2. Add wine to the remainder of the oil mixture. Then, remove it from the pan, stir veggies, and place salmon atop it all. Pour the wine mix atop it and season with remaining oregano and salt and pepper. Bake 5-10 minutes until salmon is done. Serve alongside the wedged lemon.

Walnut Crusted Salmon with Rosemary

Ingredients

- Dijon mustard (2 tsp)
- Garlic (1 clove, minced)
- Honey (0.5 tsp)
- Kosher salt (0.5 tsp)
- Lemon juice (1 tsp)
- Lemon zest (0.25 tsp.)
- Olive oil (1 tsp)
- Olive oil spray
- Panko (3 Tbsp.)
- Red pepper (0.25 tsp)
- Rosemary (1 tsp, chopped)

- Salmon (1 pound, skin removed)
- Walnuts (3 Tbsp., finely chopped)
- Parsley and lemon to garnish

Instructions

1. Mix together the mustard, lemon zest and juice, honey, salt and red pepper, and rosemary. In a separate dish, combine the panko with oil and walnuts.
2. Spread mustard across salmon and top with panko mixture. Spray fillets with cooking spray.
3. Cook until fish begins to flake at 425F, roughly 8-10 minutes. Serve with lemon and parsley.

Spaghetti and Clams

Ingredients

- Clams (6.5 lbs.)
- Olive oil (6 Tbsp.)
- White wine (0.5 c.)
- Garlic (3 cloves, sliced)
- Chiles (3, small and crumbled)
- Spaghetti (1 lb.)
- Parsley (3 Tbsp., chopped)
- Salt and pepper to personal preference

Instructions

1. Prepare clams, soaking in clean water and brushing to remove all sand.

2. Warm 2 Tbsp. of oil in large pot. Then, toss in 0.25 c. wine, 1 of the cloves of garlic, and 1 chile. Cook half of the plans at high heat with regular shaking until clams are opened. Remove opened clams and their juices to a larger bowl. Repeat process with second half of clams. Discard any that do not open.
3. Prepare pasta according to packaging to create al dente pasta. Reserve 1 c. pasta water.
4. Warm remainder of oil (2 Tbsp.) in pot over moderate heat, tossing in remainder of garlic and chile. Cook until fragrant, then place all clams and their juices into the pot, tossing to coat well. Then, toss in pasta, mixing well to combine. If necessary, add in cooking liquid. Serve and season with salt/pepper to personal preference with parsley atop.

Braised Lamb and Fennel

Ingredients

- Bay leaves (2)
- Chicken broth (3 c.)
- Cinnamon stick (1)
- Fennel (1 bulb, chopped)
- Garlic head (chopped in half)
- Lamb shoulder (3 lbs., cut into 8 pieces)
- Olive oil (2 Tbsp.)
- Onion (1, chopped
- Orange (1 with peel, cut into wedges)
- White wine (1 c.)
- Whole peeled tomatoes (14.5 oz. can)

Instructions

1. Dry lamb and season with salt and pepper to taste. Warm oil inside a Dutch oven, and sear lamb on all sides, roughly 6 minutes each side. Move lamb to plate.
2. Place fennel, garlic, and onion in the pot and cook, until browning, roughly 8 minutes. Mix in wine and boil, deglazing the pan. Reduce heat and simmer until it has reduced 50%.
3. Toss in orange, bay leaves, tomatoes, broth, and cinnamon, plus the lamb. Simmer, then cover pot and transfer to oven set to 325F. braise for 1.5-2 hours. Remove lamb and place on clean plate.
4. Strain liquid left in pot, then return it to the pot to boil until thick, roughly 30 minutes.
5. Return lamb to pot to warm. Serve.

Mediterranean Cod

Ingredients

- Black olives (0.66 c., sliced)
- Cod (4 fillets, skinless)
- Fennel seeds (1 tsp)
- Lemon (1, sliced)
- Lemon (juice of ½ lemon)
- Olive oil (6 Tbsp.)
- Onion (1, sliced)
- Parsley (1 Tbsp., chopped)
- Salt and pepper to personal preference
- Tomatoes (0.66 c., diced)

Instructions

1. Warm olive oil at a moderate temperature, sautéing the onion with a pinch of salt until translucent, roughly 10 minutes.
2. Mix in tomato and olives, tossing in the juice as well. Allow it to simmer gently for roughly 5 minutes. Toss in fennel seeds and set aside.
3. Warm the rest of the oil in another pan and fry up the cod for 10 minutes, flipping halfway through until done.
4. Toss tomato sauce over heat to warm, then mix together the parsley, and serve atop the cod with a lemon slice.

Baked Feta with Olive Tapenade

Ingredients

- Baked pita or crusty bread to serve
- Feta cheese (6 oz.)
- Garlic (2 cloves)
- Green olives (0.33 c., sliced)
- Harissa paste (3 Tbsp.)
- Olive oil (3 Tbsp.)
- Parsley (3 Tbsp., fresh chopped)
- Roasted red peppers (16-oz. jar, drained)
- Salt (0.75 tsp.)
- Tomato paste (2 Tbsp.)
- Walnuts (0.5 c., halved)

Instructions

1. In a blender, combine your peppers, 0.25 c. walnuts, harissa and tomato paste, garlic, and 0.5 tsp of your salt until mostly consistent. It doesn't have to be perfect, but should be well combined.
2. Take half of mixture into baking dish that has been sprayed with cooking spray. Top with half of your feta, then spoon the rest of the red pepper sauce atop it.
3. Top with the last of the feta and bake until bubbly, roughly 25 minutes. Broil for the last 2.
4. While that bakes, make your tapenade. This requires you to combine your remaining ingredients together.
5. Remove mixture from oven and top with tapenade. Serve immediately with crusty bread or pita chips.

Chapter 5: 30-Minutes or Less Meals

Vegetarian Toss Together Mediterranean Pasta Salad

Ingredients

- Artichoke hearts (12 oz. jar, drained)
- Balsamic vinegar (2 Tbsp.)
- Kalamata olives (12-ounce jar, drained and chopped)
- Olive oil (2 Tbsp.)
- Pasta (8 oz., wheat)
- Salt to personal preference
- Sun-dried tomatoes in oil (1.5 oz. jar, drained)

Instructions

1. Prepare pasta according to packaging.
2. Mix together olives, tomatoes, and artichoke.
3. Drain pasta and add them to a bowl with artichoke mixture. Then, top with vinegar and olive oil, mix well, and serve warm.

Vegetarian Aglio e Olio and Broccoli

Ingredients

- Olive oil (3 Tbsp.)
- Cayenne peppers (3)
- Garlic (3 cloves, sliced)
- Broccoli (1 head, prepared in florets)
- Spaghetti (7 oz. whole wheat)
- Salt to taste

Instructions

1. Boil water and prepare spaghetti according to instructions until al dente. Drain and reserve.
2. In a pan, heat up 1 Tbsp. of your olive oil at a moderate temperature, then toss in the garlic and peppers, sautéing until fragrant. Remove garlic from heat and set aside.
3. Toss broccoli into pan and cook for 4 minutes. Then toss in spaghetti, garlic, and remaining oil. Cook for an additional minute or two, then serve.

Cilantro and Garlic Baked Salmon

Ingredients

- Cilantro (stems trimmed)
- Garlic (4 cloves, chopped)
- Lime (0.5, cut into rounds)
- Lime juice (1 lime's worth)
- Olive oil (0.5 c.)
- Salmon fillet (2 pounds, skin removed)
- Salt to taste
- Tomato (cut into rounds)

Instructions

1. Allow salmon to come to room temp for 20 minutes while oven preheats to a temperature of 425 F.
2. While you wait, take a processor and combine garlic, cilantro, lime juice, and olive oil with a pinch of salt. Combine well.
3. Place fillet into baking pan that has been greased. Top with a light sprinkle of salt and pepper. Then spread cilantro sauce atop fillet, coating whole salmon. Top with tomato and lime.
4. Bake for 6 minutes per 0.5 inch of thickness (1-inch fillets take around 8-10 minutes). Let rest for 5-10 minutes out of the oven. Serve.

Harissa Pasta

Ingredients

- Pasta (2 cups)
- Red bell pepper (1)
- Red onion (1)
- Pine nuts (2 Tbsp.)
- Harissa paste (2 Tbsp.)

Instructions

1. Roast onions and peppers with olive oil at 400F for 20 minutes. Remove from oven and dice.
2. Prepare pasta to instructions on package. While pasta cooks, toast your pine nuts until browned in frying pan.
3. Drain pasta, leaving a touch of the water. Then, add in diced roasted veggies and harissa. Serve topped with pine nuts.

Chapter 6: 1-Hour-or-Less Meals

1 Hour Baked Cod

Ingredients

- Basil (0.5 tsp., dried)
- Bay leaf (1)
- Capers (1 small jar)
- Cod fillets (2 pounds)
- Fennel seeds (1 tsp., crushed)
- Garlic (1 clove, minced)
- Lemon juice (0.25 c., fresh)
- Olive oil (2 tsp)
- Onion (1, sliced)
- Orange juice (o.25 c., fresh)
- Orange peel (1 Tbsp.)
- Oregano (0.5 tsp., dried)
- Salt and pepper to personal preference
- White wine (1 c., dry)
- Whole tomatoes (16-oz. can, chopped and reserving juice)

Instructions

1. Warm oven to 375F.
2. In cast iron skillet, warm oil. Then, sauté your onion for 5 minutes. At this point, mix in all other ingredients but fish. Allow to simmer for 30 minutes.
3. Place fillets into skillet and top with most of the sauce. Allow to bake for 15 minutes until fish flakes.

Grilled Chicken Mediterranean Salad

Ingredients

- Artichoke hearts (0.33 c., chopped)
- Balsamic vinegar (2 Tbsp.)
- Basil (1 tsp, dried)
- Chicken breasts (3, cut into bite-sized chunks)
- Cucumber (0.75 c., diced)
- Feta cheese (0.25 c.)
- Garlic (1 clove, minced)
- Greek yogurt (2 Tbsp.)
- Green onions (0.25 c., chopped)

- Kalamata olives (3 Tbsp., sliced)
- Kosher salt (0.5 tsp)
- Lemon juice (3 Tbsp + 1 tsp.)
- Olive oil (3 Tbsp. + 2 Tbsp.)
- Onion powder (0.5 tsp)
- Parsley (0.5 tsp)
- Pesto (4 tsp)
- Pinch of red pepper
- Roasted red pepper (6 Tbsp., sliced)
- Romaine (4 c., chopped)
- Shiitake mushrooms
- Spinach (4 c., chopped)
- Tomato (0.75 c., diced)
- White wine vinegar (4 tsp)

Instructions

1. Create your salad. Each plate should have a bed of romaine and spinach, topped with cucumber, tomato, artichoke, peppers, olives, and cheese.
2. Combine your tsp of lemon juice, wine vinegar, and pesto in a jar and shake to combine. Then, add in yogurt and 2 Tbsp. oil, mixing well until well-incorporated.
3. Prepare your chicken. Let it marinade in a mixture of 3 Tbsp. lemon juice, balsamic vinegar, remaining oil, and all seasonings for at least 30 minutes. Soak some wooden skewers in water during this time.
4. Make kebabs out of chicken and mushroom, alternating bite of chicken and bite of mushroom until chicken is gone. Grill for 10 to 15 minutes until done.
5. Drizzle salad with the vinaigrette, then place a kebab atop each. Serve.

Lemon Herb Chicken and Potatoes One Pot Meal

Ingredients

- Baby potatoes (8, halved)
- Basil (3 tsp, dried)
- Bell pepper (1, seeds removed and wedged)
- Chicken thighs (4, skin and bone on)
- Garlic (4 large cloves, crushed)
- Kalamata olives (4 Tbsp., pitted)
- Lemon juice (1 lemon's worth)
- Olive oil (3 Tbsp.)
- Oregano (2 tsp, dried)

- Parsley (2 tsp, dried)
- Red onion (wedged)
- Red wine vinegar (1 Tbsp.)
- Salt (2 tsp)
- Zucchini (1 large, sliced)
- Lemons for garnish

Instructions

1. Combine juice from lemon, 2 Tbsp. olive oil, vinegar, seasonings, and garlic into dish. Pour half to reserve for later, then place chicken in half. Let sit for 15 minutes (or overnight if you would like to prep the day before)
2. Warm oven to 430F. Sear chicken in cast iron skillet in remaining olive oil, about 4 minutes per side. Drain all but 1 Tbsp. of fat.
3. Place all veggies around the thighs. Top with remaining marinade and combine well to cover everything.
4. Cover pan and bake for 35 minutes until soft and chicken is to temperature. Then, broil for 5 minutes or until golden brown. Top with olives and lemon to serve.

Vegetarian Mediterranean Quiche

Ingredients

- Butter (2 Tbsp.)
- Cheddar cheese (1 c., shredded)
- Eggs (4 large)
- Feta (0.33 c.)
- Garlic (2 cloves, minced)
- Kalamata olives (0.25 c., sliced)
- Milk (1.25 c.)
- Onion (1, diced)
- Oregano (1 tsp, dried)
- Parsley (1 tsp, dried)
- Pie crust (1, prepared)
- Red pepper (1, diced)
- Salt and pepper to personal preference
- Spinach (2 c., fresh)
- Sun dried tomatoes (0.5 c.)

Instructions

1. Soak sun-dried tomatoes in boiling water for 5 minutes before draining and chopping.
2. Prepare a pie dish with a crust, fluting the edges.
3. In a skillet, melt your butter, then cook your garlic and onions in it until they become fragrant. Combine in the red peppers for another 3 minutes until softened. Then, toss in your spinach, olives, and seasoning. Cook until the spinach wilts, about 5 minutes. Take it off of the heat and toss

in your feta and tomatoes. Then, carefully place mixture into the crust, spreading it into a nice, even layer.

4. Mix milk, eggs, and half of cheddar cheese together. Pour it into the crust. Then, top with cheddar.

5. Bake for 50 minutes at 375 f. until crust is browned and egg is done.

Herbed Lamb and Veggies

Ingredients

- Bell pepper (2, any color, seeds removed and cut into bite-sized chunks)
- Lamb cutlets (8 lean)
- Mint (2 Tbsp., fresh, chopped)
- Olive oil (1 Tbsp.)
- Red onion (1, wedged)
- Sweet potato (1 large, peeled, and chunked)
- Thyme (1 Tbsp., fresh, chopped)
- Zucchini (2, chunked)

Instructions

1. Assemble your veggies onto a baking sheet and coat with oil and black pepper. Bake at 400F for 25 minutes.
2. As veggies bake, trim fat from the lamb. Then, combine the herbs with a bit of freshly ground pepper. Coat the lamb in the seasoning.
3. Remove veggies, flip, and push to one side of pan. Then, arrange your cutlets onto the baking pan as well. Bake for 10 minutes, flip, then cook an additional 10 minutes. Combine well, then serve.

Chicken and Couscous Mediterranean Wraps

Ingredients

- Parsley (1 c., fresh and chopped)
- Olive oil (3 Tbsp.)

- Garlic (2 tsp, minced)
- Salt (pinch)
- Pepper (pinch)
- Chicken tenders (1 pound)
- Tomato (1, chopped)
- Cucumber (1, chopped)
- Spinach wraps (4 1o-inch)
- Water (0.5 c)
- Mint (0.5 c., fresh chopped)
- Lemon juice (0.25 c.)
- Couscous (0.33 c.)

Instructions

1. Cook couscous in boiling water according to directions on package.
2. Mix together your lemon juice, oil, garlic, salt and pepper, mint, and parsley.
3. Coat chicken in 1 Tbsp. of your mixture from previous step and top with a pinch of salt. Cook in skillet until completely cooked, usually just a few minutes per side.
4. Wait for chicken to cool, then chop into bites.
5. Pour the remainder of your parsley mixture into the couscous with cucumbers and tomato bits.
6. Place 0.75 c. of couscous mixture into a tortilla, then spread chicken atop it, rolling them up and serving.

Sheet Pan Shrimp

Ingredients

For shrimp

- Feta cheese (0.5 c.)
- Fingerling potatoes (2 c., halved)
- Green beans (6 oz., trimmed)

- Olive oil (3 Tbsp.)
- Pepper (1 tsp)
- Red onion (1 medium, sliced)
- Red pepper (1 medium, sliced)
- Salt (1 tsp)
- Shrimp (1 lb., deveined and peeled)

For Marinade

- Garlic (1 Tbsp., minced)
  Oregano (0.5 tsp)
- Greek yogurt (1 c.)
- Lemon juice (2 Tbsp.)
- Paprika (0.5 tsp)
- Parsley (2 Tbsp., chopped)

Instructions

1. Combine all marinade ingredients and set aside.
2. Take shrimp in a bowl with 0.5 c. of the marinade. Let them sit for 30 minutes.
3. During rest time, set up your baking sheet with foil or parchment, and prepare your veggies. Chop them up and toss onto baking sheet, drizzling them with the olive oil and giving them a quick sprinkle of salt and pepper. Bake for roughly 20 minutes at 400F, then remove from oven. Take out all green beans and set to the side.
4. Place shrimp in one layer across the pan and bake for an additional 10 minutes until shrimp is done. Serve with veggies and shrimp in bowls, topped with 2 Tbsp. feta and a spoonful of yogurt marinade.

Mediterranean Mahi Mahi

Ingredients

- Basil (6 leaves, freshly chopped)
- Capers (4 Tbsp.)
- Garlic (2 cloves, chopped)
- Italian seasoning (pinch)
- Kalamata olives (25, chopped)
- Lemon juice (1 tsp)
- Mahi mahi (1 pound)
- Olive oil (2 Tbsp.)
- Onion (0.5, chopped)
- Parmesan cheese (3 Tbsp.)
- Diced tomatoes (15 oz. can)
- White wine (0.25 c.)

Instructions

1. Warm olive oil in a pan and then cook onions until translucent. Toss in garlic and seasoning and stir to mix well. Then, add in your can of tomatoes, wine, olives, lemon, and roughly half of the chopped basil. Drop heat down and toss in parmesan cheese. Cook until bubbling.
2. Put fish into a baking pan, then top with the sauce. Bake for 20 minutes at 425 F until fish is to temperature.

Chapter 7: Slow Cooker Meals

Slow Cooker Mediterranean Chicken

Ingredients

- Bay leaf (1)
- Capers (1 Tbsp.)
- Chicken broth (0.5 c.)

- Chicken thighs (2 pounds, bone and skin removed)
- Garlic (3 cloves, minced)
- Kalamata olives (1 c.)
- Olive oil (1 Tbsp.)
- Oregano (1 tsp)
- Roasted red pepper (1 c.)
- Rosemary (1 tsp, dried)
- Salt and pepper to taste
- Sweet onion (1, thinly sliced)
- Thyme (1 tsp, dried)
- Optional fresh lemon wedges to juice for serving

Instructions

1. Sauté the chicken in olive oil to brown on both sides, then remove it from the pan. Then, sauté the onions and garlic as well until beginning to soften, roughly 5 minutes.
2. Put chicken, onion, garlic, and all other ingredients into a slow cooker and leave it to cook for 4 hours on low. Season to taste.

Slow Cooker Vegetarian Mediterranean Stew

Ingredients

- Carrot (0.75 c., chopped)
- Chickpeas (15 oz. can)
- Crushed red pepper (0.5 tsp)
- Fire-roasted diced tomatoes (2 14-oz. cans)
- Garlic (4 cloves, minced)
- Ground pepper (0.25 tsp)
- Kale (8 c., chopped)
- Lemon juice (1 Tbsp.)

- Olive oil (3 Tbsp.)
- Onion (1, chopped)
- Oregano (1 tsp)
- Salt (0.75 tsp)
- Vegetable broth (3 c.)
- Basil leaves (garnish)
- Lemon wedges (garnish)

Instructions

1. Mix tomatoes, onion, carrot, broth, seasonings, and garlic into the slow cooker. Cook on low for 6 hours.
2. Take out 0.25 c. of the liquid in the slow cooker after 6 hours and transfer it to a bowl. Take out 2 Tbsp. of chickpeas and mash them with the liquid until nice and smooth.
3. Combine mash, kale, juice from lemon, and whole chickpeas. Cook for about 30 minutes, until kale is tender, then serve garnished with the basil leaves and lemon wedges.

Vegetarian Slow Cooker Quinoa

Ingredients

- Arugula (4 c.)
- Chickpeas (1 15.5 oz. can, rinsed and drained)
- Feta cheese (0.5 c)
- Garlic (2 cloves, minced)
- Kalamata olives (12, halved)
- Kosher salt (0.75 tsp)
- Lemon juice (2 tsp)
- Olive oil (2.25 Tbsp.)
- Oregano (2 Tbsp., fresh and coarsely chopped

- Quinoa (1.5 c., uncooked)
- Red onion (1 c., sliced)
- Roasted red pepper (0.5 c., drained and chopped)
- Vegetable stock (2.25 c.)

Instructions

1. Mix your broth with the onion, garlic, quinoa, chickpeas, and 1.5 tsp of olive oil. Sprinkle half of the salt atop it. Mix and cook on low until quinoa is done, roughly 3 or 4 hours.
2. Turn off the slow cooker and mix well. In a separate bowl, combine remaining olive oil, salt, and lemon juice together. Then, mix that into the slow cooker, along with the peppers.
3. Combine in the arugula and leave until the greens start to wilt. Serve, topping with feta, oregano, and olives.

Slow-Cooked Chicken and Chickpea Soup

Ingredients

- Artichoke hearts (14 oz. can, drained and chopped)
- Bay leaf (1)
- Cayenne (0.25 tsp)
- Chicken thighs (2 lbs., skins removed)
- Cumin (4 tsp)
- Diced tomatoes (1 15-ounce can)
- Dried chickpeas (1.5 c., allow to soak overnight)
- Garlic cloves (4, chopped)
- Olives (o.25 c., halved)
- Paprika (4 tsp)
- Pepper (0.25 tsp)
- Salt (0.5 tsp)

- Tomato paste (2 Tbsp.)
- Water (4 c.)
- Yellow onion (chopped)
- Parsley or cilantro (garnish)

Instructions

1. Drain your soaked chickpeas and place them into your slow cooker (large preferred). Mix in the water, onions and garlic, tomatoes (undrained), tomato paste, and all seasonings. Combine well, then add in the chicken.
2. Leave it to cook for 8 hours at low, or 4 at high.
3. Remove the chicken and allow it to cool on a cutting board. At the same time, remove the bay leaf, then add in the artichoke and olives. Season with additional salt if necessary to taste. Chop up chicken, removing the bones, and then mix it back into the soup. Serve the soup with the parsley or cilantro garnishing the top.

Slow Cooked Brisket

Ingredients

- Beef broth (0.5 c.)
- Brisket (3 lbs.)
- Cold water (0.25 c.)
- Fennel bulbs (2, cored, trimmed, and cut into wedges)
- Flour
- Italian seasoning (3 tsp)
- Italian seasoning diced tomatoes (14.5 oz. can)
- Lemon peel (1 tsp., fine shreds)
- Olives (0.5 c.)
- Parsley for garnish
- Pepper (pinch)
- Salt (pinch)

Instructions

1. Trim meat, then season with 1 tsp Italian seasoning. Put it in slow cooker with the cut-up fennel on top.
2. Mix together the tomatoes, broth, peel, olives, salt and pepper, and the last of the Italian seasoning.
3. Cook at low for 10 hours, or high for 5.
4. Take meat out of the cooker and reserve all juice. Arrange meat with veggies on a serving platter.
5. Remove fat from top of the juices.
6. Take 2 c. of juices in saucepan. Mix together water and flour, then combine it into the juice. Cook until gravy forms.
7. Serve meat topped with gravy and garnish with parsley.

Vegan Bean Soup with Spinach

Ingredients

- Vegetable broth (3 14-oz. cans)
- Tomato puree (15 oz. can)
- Great Northern or White beans (15 oz. can)
- White rice (0.5 c)
- Onion (0.5 c., chopped)
- Garlic (2 cloves, minced)
- Basil (1 tsp., dried)
- Pinch of salt
- Pinch of pepper
- Kale or spinach (8 c., chopped)

Instructions

1. Mix everything but leafy greens together in your slow cooker. Cook for 5 or 7 hours on low, or 2.5 hours on high.
2. Toss in leafy greens. Wait for them to wilt and serve.

Moroccan Lentil Soup

Ingredients

- Carrots (2 c., chopped)
- Cauliflower (3 c.)
- Cinnamon (0.25 tsp)
- Cumin (1 tsp)
- Diced tomato (28 oz.)
- Fresh cilantro (0.5 c.)
- Fresh spinach (4 c.)
- Garlic (4 cloves, minced)
- Ground coriander (1 tsp)
- Lemon juice (2 Tbsp.)
- Lentils (1.75 c.)

- Olive oil (2 tsp)
- Onion (2 c., chopped)
- Pepper (pinch)
- Tomato paste (2 Tbsp.)
- Turmeric (1 tsp)
- Vegetable broth (6 c.)
- Water (2 c.)

Instructions

1. Mix everything but spinach, cilantro, and lemon juice. Cook until lentils soften. This will be 4-5 hours if you use high heat, or 10 hours on low.
2. Mix spinach when just 30 minutes remains on cook time.
3. Just before serving, top with cilantro and lemon juice.

Chapter 8: Vegetarian and Vegan Meals

Vegetarian Greek Stuffed Mushrooms

Ingredients

- Cherry tomatoes (0.5 c., quartered)
- Feta cheese (0.33 c.)
- Garlic (1 clove, mixed)
- Ground pepper (0.5 tsp)
- Kalamata olives (2 Tbsp.)
- Olive oil (3 Tbsp.)
- Oregano (1 Tbsp., fresh and roughly chopped)
- Portobello mushrooms (4, cleaned with stems and gills taken out)
- Salt (0.25 tsp)
- Spinach (1 c., chopped)

Instructions

1. Begin by setting your oven. This recipe requires 400F for baking.
2. Mix together your salt and 0.25 tsp pepper, garlic, and 2 Tbsp. of oil, and use it to cover your mushrooms, inside and out.
3. Set the mushrooms onto your baking pan and allow it to cook for 10 minutes.
4. Mix together your remaining ingredients and combine well. Then, when the mushrooms are done, remove them from the oven and then fill them up with your filling.
5. Allow to cook for another 10 minutes.

Vegetarian Cheesy Artichoke and Spinach Stuffed Squash

Ingredients

- Artichoke Hearts (10 oz., frozen—thawed and chopped up)
- Baby spinach (5 oz.)
- Cream cheese (4 oz., softened)
- Parmesan cheese (0.5 c.)
- Pepper (pinch to taste)
- Red pepper and basil (for garnish)

- Salt (pinch to taste)
- Spaghetti squash (1, cut in half and cleaned out of seeds)
- Water (3 Tbsp.)

Instructions

1. Microwave your squash, flat side down, with 2 Tbsp. of your water uncovered for 10-15 minutes.
2. Mix together your spinach and water into a skillet until they begin to wilt. Then drain and reserve for later.
3. Preheat your oven set to broil with the rack at the upper 1/3 point.
4. Remove flesh from squash with a fork, then place the shells onto a sheet for the oven. Then stir in your artichoke, cheeses, and a pinch of salt and pepper to the squash flesh. Combine thoroughly, then split it between the two shells. Broil for 3 minutes and top with red pepper and basil to taste.

Vegan Mediterranean Buddha Bowl

Ingredients

For the chickpeas

- Chickpeas (1 can, rinsed, drained, and skinned)
- Olive oil (1 tsp)
- Pinch of salt and pepper
- Dried basil (0.25 tsp)
- Garlic powder (0.25 tsp)

For the quinoa

- Quinoa (0.5 c.)
- Water (1 c.)

For the salad

- Bell pepper (1, color of choice, seeded, stemmed, and chopped to bite-sized bits)
- Cucumbers (2, peeled and chopped)
- Grape tomatoes (1 c., halved)
- Hummus (0.5 c.)
- Kalamata olives (0.5 c.)
- Lettuce (2 c. – can sub in field greens, spinach, kale, or any other leafy greens)

Instructions

1. Set your oven up to prepare for baking. It should be at 0400F. Then, mix the ingredients for the chickpeas together, coating them evenly with the seasoning.
2. Put chickpeas in single layer and put them onto the baking sheet. Roast for 30 minutes with an occasional mixing and rotation of the pan to allow them all to cook evenly. Allow them to cool.
3. Start preparing the quinoa and water in a microwave-safe bowl. Combine the water and quinoa and microwave, covered, for 4 minutes. Then stir and microwave for 2 minutes longer. Give it one final stir and leave it to rest in the microwave for another minute or two.
4. Begin assembling your salad. Begin with the greens at the bottom, then top with tomatoes, cucumbers, bell pepper, olives, chickpeas, and then quinoa. Finally, top with a dollop of hummus to serve.

Vegan Mediterranean Pasta

Ingredients

- Artichokes (0.5 c.)
- Basil leaves (0.25 c., torn)
- Garlic cloves (2-3 to taste, minced)
- Grape tomatoes (2 c., halved)
- Kalamata olives (10, pitted)
- Olive oil (1 Tbsp.)

- Pasta (8 oz.)
- Red pepper (0.25 tsp.)
- Salt and pepper to taste
- Spinach (4 c.)
- Tomato paste (4 Tbsp.)
- Vegetable broth (1 c.)

Instructions

1. Prepare your pasta based on the instructions provided. Keep 1 c. of the water for later use and then set the pasta aside.
2. While preparing your pasta, take the time to warm a large skillet with oil. Then, sauté your garlic and red pepper for 30 seconds or so. Combine in the tomato paste and cook for another minute. At that point, mix in your tomatoes, your seasoning, your artichokes and olives, and your broth. Let it cook until tomatoes start to break down.
3. Mix in the pasta to the tomato mixture. Let it cook another 2 minutes and add reserved pasta water if too dry.
4. Add in spinach and basil and cook until wilted.
5. Remove from heat and serve.

Vegetarian Zucchini Lasagna Rolls

Ingredients

- Basil (2 Tbsp., fresh)
- Egg (1, lightly beaten)
- Frozen spinach (10-ounce package, thawed and dried)
- Garlic (1 clove)
- Marinara sauce (0.75 c.)
- Olive oil (2 tsp)
- Parmesan cheese (3 Tbsp.)
- Pinch each of salt and pepper
- Ricotta (1.33 c.)
- Shredded mozzarella cheese (8 Tbsp.)
- Zucchini (2, trimmed)

Instructions

1. Prepare two baking sheets with cooking spray. Then set the oven to 425F.
2. Cut up your zucchini into strips lengthwise into 1/8 inch thick pieces. A mandolin will make this easier.
3. Prepare zucchini coated in oil with salt and pepper, then set up a flat layer across the bottom of the prepared pan.
4. Bake zucchini for 10 minutes until it begins to soften.
5. Mix together 2 Tbsp. mozzarella and 1 Tbsp. of parmesan. Then, in another bowl, combine egg, ricotta, spinach, garlic, and the remainder of the cheese. Toss in a pinch of salt and pepper and mix well.
6. Set up an 8-inch square casserole dish with 0.25 c. marinara spread across the bottom.
7. Take your zucchini that has been softened and begin to roll it. To do this, you will need to put 1 Tbsp. of ricotta mix at the bottom of your strip, then roll. Put the seam down in the marinara-covered bottom. Do this for all pieces of zucchini.
8. Cover the rolls with the remainder of your marinara sauce and top with the cheese mix.
9. Bake until bubbling, roughly 20 minutes. Rest for 5 minutes and top with basil.

Vegetarian Breakfast Sandwich

Ingredients

- Sandwich thins (2)
- Olive oil (2 Tbsp. + 1 tsp)
- Rosemary (1 Tbsp. fresh, or 0.5 tsp dried)

- Eggs (2)
- Spinach leaves (1 c.)
- Tomato (0.5, sliced thinly)
- Feta (2 Tbsp.)
- Pinch of salt and pepper

Instructions

1. Warm oven to 375F. Separate your sandwich thins and coat with olive oil. Bake for 5 minutes until beginning to crisp up.
2. Warm skillet with last tsp of olive oil. Break eggs into pan and cook until whites are set. Then, break the yolks and flip to finish cooking.
3. Put bottoms of the bread onto serving plates. Then, top with spinach, the tomato, one egg each, followed by the feta. Sprinkle with salt and pepper, then top with remaining bread.

Vegan Breakfast Toast

Ingredients

- Bread of choice (verify that it is vegan—2 slices)
- Spice blend of choice
- Arugula (handful)
- Tomato (1, cut into rounds)
- Chopped olives (1 Tbsp.)
- Cucumber (0.5, cut into rounds)
- Hummus (0.25 c.)

Instructions

1. Toast up your bread. Then spread the hummus across, season it, and top with all toppings split between the pieces.

Vegetarian Shakshouka

Ingredients

- Chopped parsley (1 Tbsp.)
- Diced Tomatoes (15 oz. can)
- Eggs (4)
- Garlic (2 cloves)

- Olive oil (2 Tbsp.)
- Onion (1—sliced)
- Red bell peppers (2, sliced thinly)
- Salt and pepper to taste
- Spicy harissa (1 tsp)
- Sugar (1 tsp)

Instructions

1. Warm oil in a cast iron pan. Sauté your peppers and onions until they have begun to soften, giving them a stir every now and then to prevent sticking. Add in the garlic for another minute.
2. Put in tomatoes, sugar, and harissa, leaving it to simmer for the next 7 minutes.
3. Season it to taste. Then, add in small indentations into the mixture in the pan, cracking an egg in each indentation that you make. Cover up the pot and allow it to cook until egg whites are done.
4. Cover with parsley and serve with bread.

PART IV

Chapter 1: The Fundamentals of a Low Sugar Diet for Diabetics

For people with diabetes, eating can be quite a challenge. After all, it's not easy dealing with the various recommendations made by doctors. The fact is that the following recommended guidelines are essential to keeping your diabetes in check.

You see, it's important to ensure that your blood sugar levels remain in check. One of the easiest and most effective ways to do this is by keeping your sugar and carb intake as low as possible. So, let's take a look at how this occurs when you go on the low-sugar and low-carb, diabetic diet.

Firstly, when you consume carbs and sugars, these are converted into glucose in the bloodstream as the liver metabolizes them. Since carbs are used as a source of energy, the body needs to secrete insulin from the pancreas in order to break down glucose and send it into the cells as functional energy. Then, the body mixes oxygen to create ATP. This is the source of energy that helps you power your body's entire system.

All is good until there is an excess of glucose in the body. When this occurs, the body stores excess glucose as fat. However, there comes a point where the body just can't keep up. This is where insulin resistance happens. In a nutshell, your cells simply stop accepting any more glucose as there is simply too much glucose in the bloodstream.

These are the spikes in blood sugar levels.

This is where the low-carb, low-sugar diet makes a huge difference in your overall health management plan. The rationale is that when you restrict the number of carbs and sugar that you consume, you are basically giving your body the chance to process what's already in the bloodstream and in storage. So, you are creating a deficit that forces the body to use up what it's already stored.

This is how you can get your blood sugar levels in check.

In a manner of speaking, what you are doing is giving your body a break. Therefore, the body has a chance to catch up. When your body eventually catches up, you end up reducing your overall blood sugar levels. In addition, medication is much more effective as there are fewer carbs and glucose to process.

At first, it can be a bit of a psychological shock to think that you have to go on a low-carb, low-sugar diet. In fact, most people think they have to live on lettuce for the rest of their lives. What you will find is that this diet embraces a large number of foods that are very low in carbs and sugar. As a result, you can eat healthy and tasty at the same time.

However, the secret is knowing which foods promote low blood sugar levels. When you discover these foods, you'll find that keeping your diabetes in check doesn't have to be tough. You can still enjoy delicious foods with zero guilt.

Now that's a plan!

Chapter 2: Benefits of a Low Sugar Diet for Diabetics

The low-sugar, low-carb diet is filled with a number of benefits that diabetics can obtain. The best part is that you don't need to wait for an extended period of time to see the benefits. In fact, you can see benefits within a few days of trying out the diet. This is what makes the diet itself so encouraging.

So, here is a list of five benefits you can expect when going on the low-sugar diet.

1. **Reduction in blood sugar levels**

Naturally, this is the most immediate benefit of this diet. As mentioned earlier, when you reduce the amount of carbs and sugar, your body will begin to use up what's already stored in the system. This is why you can begin to see a reduction in your blood sugar levels within a few days. Over time, your blood sugar levels will begin to normalize. So, the diet, along with medication, will prove to be quite effective.

2. Weight loss

Another benefit is weight loss. Since the body converts glucose into fat when it's stored, a reduction in your carb and sugar consumption will force your body to convert stored fat into energy. This is why folks who go on the low-carb diet begin to see weight loss after a few weeks. While this result isn't immediate, it is almost certain that you'll see weight loss, especially if you are overweight.

3. Increased levels of energy

One of the symptoms that accompany diabetes is low levels of energy. This is due to the imbalance that occurs in the metabolism. Since the metabolism cannot keep up with the amount of carbs and sugar in the bloodstream, it does not produce energy as efficiently as it could. As a result, there are lower levels of energy. When you essentially force your body to process stored up fat, your metabolism becomes more efficient in producing energy. The end result is a boost in energy levels. So, don't be surprised if you find at you feel more energetic after a few days.

4. Hormonal regulation

Hormones tend to go out of whack when there are increased levels of blood sugar. For instance, insulin is the first hormone that goes haywire. However, other hormones are affected as well, such as cortisol (it is associated with weight gain) or epinephrine (used to breakdown and release nutrients in the blood). These hormones tend to work inefficiently when there is a high level of blood sugar. As a result, you may not be getting the most nutrition out of the foods you eat.

5. Improved cognitive function

Sugar, in general, works like a fuel in your body. So, when you consume a large amount of sugar, you get the rush that can power you through a given time period. However, sugar is a very poor fuel as your brain burns right through it. The end result is a severe crash afterward. Over time, your brain builds up "gunk." This gunk limits the brain's capabilities. As such, when you replace sugar with other types of fuels, such as vegetable-based carbs, then your brain produces energy more effectively. It's like putting diesel into an unleaded engine. Sure, the car will run, but it will run poorly. This is why many folks on the low-sugar diet report improved cognitive abilities, thereby reducing the phenomenon known as "brain fog."

With these benefits, you can't go wrong with the low-sugar diet!

Chapter 3: Savory Recipe Ideas

Savory Idea #1: Tangy Cabbage Treat

Number of people served: 4

Time you'll need: 33 to 37 minutes

Calories: 253

Fats: 22.8 g

Proteins: 7.9 g

Carbs: 4.7 g

What you'll require:

- Jalapeno Peppers (two, chopped)
- Cabbage (one Head)
- Pepper & salt (as preferred)
- Onion (one, chopped)
- Bacon (six, strips)

What you need to do:

1. Firstly, cook bacon as per the directions on the pack. While you allow the bacon to reach its optimal point, ready cabbage, and onions by chopping into smaller bite-sized morsels.
2. Once the bacon has been prepared to your preference, take it out of the pan and toss the onion and cabbage in. Please ensure to mix up

everything with the leftover grease from the bacon while simmering in low fire.
3. Next, get the jalapenos ready by cutting up into pieces as small as you like. Feel free to throw in with the other elements.
4. After the vegetables have reached their optimal point, take the crispy bacon and crumble over the entire mix. Add pepper & salt, along with any other low-carb or low-sugar spices.
5. Lastly, toss everything around until the entire mix is thoroughly even. Serve and enjoy!

Savory Idea #2: Low-carb Egg &Veggie Bites

Number of people served: 6

Time you'll need: 11 to 14 minutes

Calories: 21.8

Fats: 3.7 g

Proteins: 4.3 g

Carbs: 1.8 g

What you'll require:

- Bell Pepper (75 g, Chopped)
- Cucumber (45 g, Chopped)
- Spinach (225 g, Chopped)
- Tomato (75 g, Chopped)
- Eggs (three)
- Salt (as preferred)

What you need to do:

1. To get started, set up oven to 180 degrees Celsius along with a muffin tray. The smaller trays are better as they allow for smaller portions if you wish.
2. Next, use a mixing container and place eggs (cracked) inside. Whisk briskly until they are thoroughly mixed.
3. Now, coat trays with your choice of grease (for instance, non-stick spray). Please ensure to leave some extra for the vegetables (chopped)
4. Then, place eggs in the spaces in the tray and toss in vegetables are per your preference. Please make sure to stir so that the mix is distributed evenly. Then, place in the heat for roughly 11 to 14 minutes.
5. Lastly, make sure to check the mixture is cooked all the way through. Serve as a breakfast treat or yummy snack.

Savory Idea #3: Yummy Chicken Dee-light

Number of people served: 2

Time you'll need: 35 to 40 minutes

Calories: 794.7

Fats: 39.1 g

Proteins: 44.2 g

Carbs: 3.3 g

What you'll require:

- Rosemary Leaves (10 g)
- Pepper & salt (as preferred)
- Garlic (cloves, six, minced)
- Chicken Breast (455 g boneless & skinless)
- Cheddar Cheese (70 g, shredded)
- Butter (55 g)

What you need to do:

1. Firstly, set up your oven to a temperature of approximately 190 degrees Celsius. While the oven gain temperature, prepare a tray with grease (your choice).
2. Next, add seasoning to chicken to your liking.
3. Then, begin to prepare garlic butter. Take pan or skillet and set to medium fire on the range. Once the butter has thoroughly melted, toss in garlic and let cook for roughly five to six minutes. Once this time has passed, garlic should be brownish, but make sure it is not burnt. Now, cover chicken with this butter & garlic mix.
4. Once this mix is prepared, set into the oven for about ½ an hour. Make sure to check the chicken so that it is fully cooked all the way through to the center. Once this has been achieved, add cheese as a topping. Allow to melt.
5. Serve by adding some more butter & garlic mix on top. Enjoy!

Savory Idea #4: Low-carb Fried Chicken Surprise

Number of people served: 6

Time you'll need: 33 minutes

Calories: 768

Fats: 54.1 g

Proteins: 59.2 g

Carbs: 1.9 g

What you'll require:

- Pork (rinds, 85 g)
- Pepper & salt (as preferred)
- Lard (according to need)
- Egg (one)
- Chicken (thighs, six)

What you need to do:

1. First, heat up iron pan or skillet on a range top. Then, place eggs in a mixing container for whisking.
2. Next, prepare rinds by crumbling. Upon completion, coat chicken pieces with egg (you can use a brush or dip) and season as per your liking with salt & pepper.
3. Now, take covered chicken pieces and roll over in the rind crumbs. Do this for every piece.
4. After, add in about half an inch of lard (or cooking oil) into pan or skillet. Wait until it reaches the boiling point. Then, place chicken pieces into the fire. Leave for about four to six minutes on each side. Please make sure they are cooked all the way through.
5. Please ensure to turn chicken around at least twice to ensure proper cooking. Serve with a side of crispy veggies or veggie chips.

Savory Idea #5: Low-Sugar Beef Explosion

Number of people served: 4

Time you'll need: one hour

Calories: 331

Fats: 26.7 g

Proteins: 18.7 g

Carbs: 2.1 g

What you'll require:

- Garlic (cloves, two, chopped)
- Coconut grounds (55 g)
- Onions (green, three)
- Coconut Oil (45 g)
- Ginger (10 g, grated)
- Steak (Flat-iron, 455 g)

What you need to do:

1. First, get steak ready by cutting it up into long, thin slices. Upon completion, place into a large freezer bag so that you can add ginger, coconut grounds, and garlic. Then, place into refrigeration so it can marinate for about one hour's time.
2. Next, put a pan or skillet to heat. Add oil for the meat. Heat up for about three to four minutes until it is at boiling point. Then, toss in

steak and let sit until thoroughly cooked. This should take about five to seven minutes.

3. After, add in onions (green) to give the flavor a kick. Let everything sit for a minute or two until the texture is as per your liking.

4. Lastly, take some of the marinade from the freezer bag and add in right before turning off the fire. This will add an extra kick. Serve over zucchini pasta or low-carb couscous.

Savory Idea #6: Tangy Pork Extravaganza

Number of people served: 4

Time you'll need: 34 to 37 minutes

Calories: 466.1

Fats: 32.3 g

Proteins: 47.2 g

Carbs: 2.7 g

What you'll require:

- Stock (chicken, 55 g)

- Pepper (7.5 g)
- Pork (chops, four)
- Milk (202 g)
- Coriander (9 g)
- Thyme (dried, 14.5 g)
- Garlic (cloves, two, minced)
- Butter (47 g)
- Salt (14.5 g)
- Oregano (dried, 14.5 g)

What you need to do:

1. First, get chops ready by placing them on a baking sheet. Sprinkle with pepper & salt to season. Please ensure that seasoning is evenly distributed to guarantee flavor. Let sit for one hour. Once time has passed, carefully rinse chops of excess fluid.
2. Next, set the pan to high heat on range top. Place garlic & butter to stir. Once the garlic is fully transparent, the time has come to add in chops on top.
3. Once chops are placed, cook them through for roughly four to six minutes on both sides. Then, let simmer for another minute, or so, to enable flavors to combine. Remove and set aside.
4. Then, on low fire, throw in stock (chicken), and some milk. Scrape the little leftover bits from the chops. Upon completion, toss oregano, coriander, and thyme in. Please ensure you are only simmering and not boiling the sauce.
5. Lastly, as the sauce thickens, turn the heat off and toss chops back into skillet. Combine all elements and add more pepper & salt if desired. Serve with veggies or a fresh salad.

Savory Idea #7: Filet & Cheese Supreme

Number of people served: 3 or 4

Time you'll need: 31 to 36 minutes

Calories: 211

Fats: 17.4 g

Proteins: 11.9 g

Carbs: 2.25 g

What you'll require:

- Paprika (4.5 g)
- Fish Fillet (225 g)
- Parsley (flakes, 7.5 g)
- Pepper (black, 4.5 g)
- Oil (Olive, 18.5 g)
- Cheese (Parmesan, 45 g)

What you need to do:

1. First, heat up the oven to approximately 180 degrees Celsius.
2. Now, get mixing container for the pepper (black), paprika, cheese (Parmesan), and parsley.
3. Then, cover filets with the spice mix. Add oil (olive) and then rollup the mixture ensuring an even coating.
4. Once the fish is ready, set the filets on to tray and place it into the oven for roughly fourteen to seventeen minutes.
5. Lastly, double-check fish is thoroughly cooked and place cheese on top to create a crust. Let sit for a few moments, until cheese is crispy, remove, and serve. Enjoy with veggies or low-carb brown rice.

Savory Idea #8: Quick and Easy Low-carb Chips

Number of people served: 4

Time you'll need: 28 to 34 minutes

Calories: 91.7

Fats: 8.1 g

Proteins: 3.2 g

Carbs: 2.8 g

What you'll require:

- Salt (as preferred)
- Pepper (as preferred)
- Bacon (slices, eight)
- Oil (Olive, 18.5 g)

What you need to do:

1. First, set up an oven to approximately 180 degrees Celsius.
2. Next, grease a tray with oil (olive) or your choice of grease. Then, break up the bacon into small, bite-sized pieces.
3. After, season with pepper & salt as per your taste.
4. Then, throw into the oven for roughly eighteen to twenty-one minutes. Remove and let cool.
5. Once cool to touch, take bits and put into a skillet, or pan, over medium fire. This process usually takes about four to six minutes. Remove from fire and serve as chips. You can serve with a low-fat, low-carb dip as an appetizer!

Savory Idea #9: Unbelievably Low-carb South Treat

Number of people served: 3 to 4

Time you'll need: 29 to 32 minutes

Calories: 288

Fats: 22.3 g

Proteins: 18.9 g

Carbs: 2.7 g

What you'll require:

- Turkey Breast (roasted, 225 g, chopped)
- Cheese (Parmesan, 75 g)
- Cheddar Cheese (shredded, 225 g)
- White Cheddar Cheese (shredded, 225 g)

What you need to do:

1. First, set up an oven to approximately 180 degrees Celsius.
2. Next, take a mixing container and combine all cheeses. You can whisk or use an electric mixer. Then, take a spoonful of the mix and place onto baking sheet in a clump. Lay down as you would with cookies. Space clumps about one inch apart.
3. Upon filling sheet, throw into over for roughly seven to eight minutes. Please ensure that chips do not get burned. Chips are cooked thoroughly when edges turn light to a golden brown. Then, remove and let cool all the way.
4. Lastly, chop up turkey breast and serve chips with a low-sugar dip. Serve as a snack or entrée.

Savory Idea #10: Low-sugar Italian Snack Option

Number of people served: 4 to 6

Time you'll need: About 22 minutes

Calories: 226

Fats: 23.7 g

Proteins: 18.4 g

Carbs: 5.7 g

What you'll require:

- Mozzarella Cheese (shredded, 225 g)
- Pepper (as preferred)
- Seasoning (Italian, 14.5 g)
- Pepperoni (115 g, chopped)
- Garlic (powder, 8.5 g)
- Salt (as preferred)
- Additional choice: Marinara Sauce for Dipping

What you need to do:

1. First, set up an oven to approximately 180 degrees Celsius.
2. Next, take a small muffin tray and coat with spray (cooking). Leave to one side.
3. Then, in a mixing container, combine pepper & cheese, garlic (powder), salt, and seasoning (Italian). Mix cheese thoroughly and add in the

seasoning. Place spoonful of mixture into the bottom of each space on tray.
4. After, top each space with pepperoni. Once ready, place into the oven for about eight to ten minutes. After this time, the cheese should be melted all the way through and light brown around the sides.
5. Lastly, remove, let cool, and serve with low-sugar sauce (marinara works best). Serve as a snack or side for a meat dish.

Chapter 4: Gourmet Recipe Ideas

Gourmet Idea #1: Tasty Chicken and Veggie Pot

Number of people served: 4 to 6

Time you'll need: 26 to 32 minutes

Calories: 238

Fats: 10.9g

Proteins: 27.6g

Carbs: 2.7g

What you'll require:

- Broccoli (one bag, frozen)
- Chicken (115g, shredded)
- Garlic Powder (as preferred)
- Soup (Cream of Mushroom, one can)
- Pepper (as preferred)
- Cheese (Cheddar 221g)

What you need to do:

1. First, prepare the oven to approximately 185 degrees Celsius.
2. Then, in a mixing container, toss in the various elements you will be using (chicken, cheese, and spices)
3. Next, add in soup.
4. Then, place the mixture into a baking container and insert it into the oven.
5. After, let cook in the oven for about twenty-five to thirty minutes.
6. Lastly, ensure that the soup has been thoroughly cooked and cheese properly melted. Serve with a side of crispy veggies or almond breadsticks.

Gourmet Idea #2: Delicious Low-sugar Chicken Meal

Number of people served: 4

Time you'll need: Approximately 30 minutes

Calories: 384

Fats: 21.1g

Proteins: 48.1g

Carbs: 3.2g

What you'll require:

- Cream (Sour, 221 g)
- Salt (9.5 g)
- Chicken (Breast, 1kg, no bone)
- Garlic (Powder, 14.5g)
- Pepper (4.5 g)
- Cheese (Parmesan, 165g, grated)

What you need to do:

1. First, prepare the oven to approximately 185 degrees Celsius.
2. Next, prepare a baking container with grease (or your choice such as spray)
3. After, in a mixing tray, add sour cream and a cup of cheese (Parmesan)
4. Then, place the chicken (breast) into the tray while spreading the mix atop each piece. Also, cover lightly with leftover cheese.
5. After that, insert the tray into the oven. Let it sit there for about twenty-seven to twenty-nine minutes.
6. Lastly, remove once thoroughly cooked and serve with your favorite low-carb side.

Gourmet Idea #3: Italian Chicken Dinner Delight

Number of people served: 2 to 4

Time you'll need: Approximately 25 minutes

Calories: 581

Fats: 41.1g

Proteins: 48.2g

Carbs: 6.1g

What you'll require:

- Garlic (Cloves, two, Minced)
- Tomatoes (Sun-dried, 65g)
- Spinach (221g, Chopped)
- Chicken (Breast, four)
- Paprika (8.5g)
- Cream (Heavy, 221 g)
- Garlic (Powder, 8.5g)
- Butter (14.5 g)
- Salt (8.5g)

What you need to do:

1. First, combine garlic (powder), paprika, and salt into mixing container. Upon completion, use this mixture to coat chicken lightly.
2. Next, fire up a skillet, or pan, and throw in two spoonfuls of butter at the base. Let the butter melt. After this, add in properly seasoned

chicken and let cook thoroughly. This would take about five minutes per side. Please ensure chicken is cooked all the way through. Remove and place to one side.

3. Then, add in the rest of the elements: tomatoes, cream, and tomatoes. It will take about three minutes on low fire for the mix to thicken. After, toss in spinach and mix up everything for four more minutes.

4. Lastly, throw the chicken back into the mix so that all flavors can combine. Ensure that chicken is properly cooked and season further if needed. Serve with a side of veggies, zucchini pasta, or low-carb couscous.

Gourmet Idea #4: Yummy Lemon Beef Surprise

Number of people served: 4
Time you'll need: Approximately three hours

Calories: 507
Fats: 35.1g
Proteins: 44.8g
Carbs: 3.1g

What you'll require:

- Pepper (4.5g)
- Lemon (one)
- Garlic (Cloves, four, Crushed)
- Salt (4.5 g)
- Beef (one kg, Cubed)
- Parsley (26g, Minced)

What you need to do:

1. First, prepare the oven to approximately 167 degrees Celsius.
2. Then, prepare a baking container with foil lining.
3. Next, get a mixing container and cover beef (cubed) with juice (lemon), some zest (lemon), salt, and garlic as preferred. Once it is ready to taste, fold over foil to create a small package.
4. Then, when the package is ready, insert into the middle section of the oven and let sit for roughly three hours. This longer cooking time is intended to let the meat soften to its best point.
5. Lastly, remove the package and let sit for about five or six minutes. Cover meat with more juice (lemon) and sprinkle parsley on top. Serve with your favorite low-carb side.

Gourmet Idea #5: Gourmet Sirloin Option

Number of people served: 3 to 4

Time you'll need: 25 to 30 minutes

Calories: 389

Fats: 18.9g

Proteins: 47.1g

Carbs: 2.3g

What you'll require:

- Garlic (Cloves, four, Crushed)
- Oil (Olive, 12g)
- Pepper & salt (as preferred)
- Steak (Sirloin, 945g, Cubed)
- Butter (14.5 g)

What you need to do:

1. First, get an iron skillet or pan and place it on high heat and place oil (olive).
2. Next, add in pepper & salt to the steak as per your preference.
3. Once the steak has been seasoned according to your preference, place it in the hot skillet, or pan, with hot oil. Let the steak in the hot oil for about four minutes on each side. Turnover twice. Then remove. After, using the same skillet, or pan, toss in butter and garlic. Please ensure to move constantly, so the mix doesn't get burnt.
4. When the garlic is light or golden brown. Place meat for another couple of minutes on each side. Let simmer until the flavors are combined. Serve with your favorite side.

Gourmet Idea #6: Unbelievably Low-sugar Surprise

Number of people served: 4 to 6

Time you'll need: Approximately 20 minutes

Calories: 171

Fats: 11.8g

Proteins: 14.6g

Carbs: 2.9g

What you'll require:

- Cheese (Mozzarella, 100g, Shredded)
- Cheese (Parmesan, 75g, Grated)
- Cheddar Cheese (Shredded, 75g)
- Eggs (two)
- Ham (221g, Diced)

What you need to do:

1. First, set up oven to 185 degrees Celsius.
2. Next, get a mixing container so you can combine egg and the various types of cheeses (shredded). After thoroughly mixing, toss in ham (diced) and continue combining until mixture is evenly distributed.
3. After, get a baking container so it can be greased (your choice of grease).
4. Now, separate mixture into eight round balls or rolls.
5. Then, insert the baking container into the oven for approximately twenty minutes. The rolls will be ready once the cheese has melted, and a golden-brown crust has formed.
6. Lastly, remove the dish and allow it to cool. Serve with chicken or any other meat of your choice.

Gourmet Idea #7: Low-carb Salmon Delight

Number of people served: 3 to 4

Time you'll need: 18 to 24 minutes

Calories: 276

Fats: 19.1g

Proteins: 24.5g

Carbs: 3.7g

What you'll require:

- Rosemary (Fresh, two Springs)
- Lemon (55 g)
- Pepper (as preferred)
- Garlic (Cloves, three)
- Salt (4.5 g)
- Salmon (Filets, four)
- Butter (Unsalted, 8.5g)

What you need to do:

1. First, start out by setting the oven to 202 degrees Celsius.
2. Next, line baking container with a sheet of paper (parchment) and set to the side.
3. Then, rinse out filets (salmon) and pat down to try. Upon completion, place on the baking container with the skin facing down.
4. After, take some soft butter to cover the top of the filer. Also, add in some pepper & salt according to your liking.
5. Now, add the spices (rosemary) and the garlic. Cover the filet and insert it into the oven for roughly thirteen to sixteen minutes.
6. Lastly, remove the filet when thoroughly cooked. Add some juice (lemon) to add a tangy zest. Serve with a side of veggies for a nutritious meal.

Gourmet Idea #8: Shrimp-Avocado Treat

Number of people served: 4

Time you'll need: 30 to 35 minutes

Calories: 539

Fats: 45.2g

Proteins: 25.8g

Carbs: 6.1g

What you'll require:

- Onion (62.5g)
- Cooked shrimp (455g, Chopped)
- Eggs (two)
- Seasoning (Seafood, 4.5g)
- Juice (Lemon, 8.5g)
- Parsley (Fresh, 14.5g)
- Crab (Cooked 125g)
- Avocados (four)
- Cheese (Cheddar, 221 g, Shredded)

What you need to do:

1. First, start out by setting the oven to 177 degrees Celsius.
2. Then, in a mixing container, combine the ingredients: eggs, seasoning (seafood), juice (lemon), onion (chopped), cheese (cheddar), parsley, shrimp, and crab.
3. Next, as the stuffing is completed, cut up avocados in half and remove the pit. Then replace the pit with the stuffing.
4. Lastly, insert the avocados in the oven for roughly twenty-seven minutes. Remove from oven and serve with almond breadsticks.

Gourmet Idea #9: Gourmet Hot Pot Surprise

Number of people served: 4 to 6
Time you'll need: Approximately 45 minutes

Calories: 287
Fats: 20.8g
Proteins: 21.9g
Carbs: 4.8g

What you'll require:

- Cheese (Swiss, 70g, Shredded)
- Pepper (as preferred)
- Garlic (Cloves, four, Minced)
- Fish (Filet, your choice, 455g)
- Shrimp (455g)
- Cream (Heavy, 87g)
- Paprika (as preferred)
- Salt (as preferred)

What you need to do:

1. First, start out by setting the oven to 191 degrees Celsius.
2. Next, prepare a baking container with grease (your choice).
3. Then, cut the filet (fish) into small to medium-sized pieces and place them on the bottom of the baking container. Then, place a layer of shrimp on top of the fish. Add pepper & salt as per your liking.
4. After, when you have everything layered, add in garlic and heavy cream to cover. Upon liberally covering, add cheese (Swiss) on top. Add a touch of paprika for that tangy edge.
5. Now, insert into the oven for roughly sixteen to eighteen minutes. Check often to make sure it does not overcook.
6. Lastly, serve with almond bread!

Gourmet Idea #10: Low-carb Tuna Wraps Treat

Number of people served: 4

Time you'll need: About 10 minutes

Calories: 109

Fats: 5.7g

Proteins: 7.8g

Carbs: 7.1g

What you'll require:

- Yogurt (Greek, 50g)
- Wrap (Wheat, four)
- Bell Pepper (Red, 25g, Diced)
- Spinach (45g)
- Celery (65g, Diced)
- Tuna (one can)

What you need to do:

1. First, drain liquid from the can, and place tuna into a mixing container. Once this is in place, add in the red bell pepper, celery, and the Greek yogurt. Combine elements together well, so the vegetables and tuna are combined thoroughly.
2. Next, you are going to want to place the mixture into the middle of the whole-wheat wraps and top off with the spinach.
3. Serve with veggie chips and lemonade for a refreshing brunch treat.

Chapter 5: Quick and Easy Recipe Ideas

Quick and Easy Idea #1: Quick and Easy Veggie Treat

Number of people served: 4

Time you'll need: 35 to 40 minutes

Calories: 51

Fats: 3.1 g

Proteins: 4.5 g

Carbs: 2.3 g

What you'll require:

- Egg (whites, two)
- Spinach (221g, chopped)
- Eggs (whole, two)
- Pepper (Bell, one)
- Salsa (14.5g)
- Onion (35g, chopped)
- Pepper & salt (as preferred)

What you need to do:

1. First, place the pan over medium fire. Once it is warm, throw in some oil (olive) and start by placing spinach and onion until reaching consistency to your preference. Season with pepper plus salt. Add more salsa if you wish.

2. Next, let your vegetables cook, cut up a bell pepper in two slices to create a small bowl. Upon completion, add the spinach mix to the pepper bowls and the open an egg on top.

3. Then, insert into the oven for about 25 to 28 minutes. Make sure to see that egg is thoroughly prepared.

4. Lastly, serve as a side to your favorite meat dish.

Quick and Easy Idea #2: Spicy Egg and Veggie Dash

Number of people served: 12

Time you'll need: 30 to 35 minutes

Calories: 242

Fats: 21.7 g

Proteins: 10.2 g

Carbs: 1.1 g

What you'll require:

- Bacon (in strips, 11)
- Onion (Powder, 4.5g)
- Garlic (Powder, 4.5g)
- Cheese (cream, 95g)
- Pepper & salt (as preferred)
- Eggs (8)
- Peppers (Jalapeno, four, Chopped)
- Cheese (Cheddar, 121 g)

What you need to do:

1. First, fire up the oven to 165 degrees Celsius.
2. Then, fire up bacon until crispy.
3. Next, in another container, mix up chopped jalapenos, eggs, cheese (cream), and seasoning. Toss in leftover bacon grease.

4. Then, take a muffin baking container and fill the edge of each space with bacon. Upon completion, pour in the mix down the middle of each space. Fill up to about 2/3 of the way. This is important as eggs will rise.
5. After, add some cheese (cheddar) and some jalapeno to provide spice. Insert into the oven and let cook for about 22 to 24 minutes. These will be ready when eggs are thoroughly done and fluffy.
6. Lastly, remove and serve as a snack or an appetizer.

Quick and Easy Idea #3: Low-sugar Hot Cake Surprise

Number of people served: 10

Time you'll need: Approximately 20 minutes

Calories: 133

Fats: 11.8 g

Proteins: 5.3 g

Carbs: 1.9 g

What you'll require:

- Flour (Almond, 221 g)
- Eggs (4)
- Milk (Almond, Non-sugar, 36.5g)
- Extract (Vanilla, 7.5g)
- Baking Powder (4.7g)
- Oil (Olive, 18.5g)

What you need to do:

1. First, in a mixing container, mix up baking powder, extract (vanilla), milk (almond), flour (almond), and eggs. Please ensure all clumps are removed.
2. Next, use a tablespoon to place mixture into pan or skillet. Prepare these as you would regular pancakes.
3. Last, top with butter or non-sugar syrup.

Quick and Easy Idea #4: Cheesy Veggie Bites

Number of people served: 4

Time you'll need: Approximately 30 minutes

Calories: 161

Fats: 11.6 g

Proteins: 11.4 g

Carbs: 5.1 g

What you'll require:

- Flour (Almond, 36.5g)
- Onion (36.5g, minced)

- Seasoning (Mexican, 8.5g)
- Mozzarella (221g, shredded)
- Broccoli (225g)
- Salt (as preferred)
- Garlic (clove, one, minced)
- Cilantro (17.5g)
- Egg (one)
- Pepper (as preferred)

What you need to do:

1. First, set up 201 degrees Celsius.
2. Next, prepare a baking container by lining with parchment paper.
3. Then, steam broccoli in a pot (5 minutes) or microwave (1-2 minutes). Tenderize broccoli to make chopping easier.
4. After, cut up broccoli into small chunks. Throw everything into mixing container (parsley, cheese, flour, egg, and spices). Mix up thoroughly until evenly distributed.
5. Now, roll up into a small ball and distribute evenly throughout the baking container.
6. Once completed, cover with some oil (olive) and insert it into the oven for about 26 to 28 minutes.
7. Lastly, serve with low-carb dip as a snack.

Quick and Easy Idea #5: Low-carb Pudding Dee-light

Number of people served: 4

Time you'll need: 18 to 20 minutes

Calories: 132

Fats: 12.1g

Proteins: 13.8g

Carbs: 1.4g

What you'll require:
- Coconut (125g, shredded)
- Almonds (221g, chopped)
- Chia seed (221g)
- Milk (almond, 225g)

What you need to do:
1. First, measure out all of the fixings and add to the Instant Pot, stirring well.
2. Then, secure the lid and select the high setting (2-5 minutes)
3. Lastly, quick release the pressure and place the pudding into four serving glasses.

Quick and Easy Idea #6: Tangy Egg Salad

Number of people served: 4 to 5

Time you'll need: 26 to 32 minutes

Calories: 314

Fats: 25.7g

Proteins: 15.4g

Carbs: 1.4g

What you'll require:

- Bacon (strips, five, raw)
- Paprika (smoked, 14.5)
- Eggs (large, 10)
- Onion (green, 36.5g)
- Mayonnaise (125g)
- Mustard (Dijon, 45g)
- Pepper & salt (as preferred)

Also required: 6-7-inch baking container

What you need to do:
1. First, grease up all sides of the pan inside of pot on the trivet. Toss one cup of cold water in the bottom of the Instant Pot and add the steam rack.
2. Next, open up eggs in a pan.
3. Then, insert pan on rack. Secure the lid and set the timer for 6 minutes (high-pressure). Natural release the pressure to remove pan.
4. After, remove any moisture. Flip pan over on a wooden cutting board for egg loaf to release. Cut up and place it into a mixing dish.
5. Now, clean the Instant Pot container and choose the sauté function (medium fire). Prepare bacon till crispy.
6. After that, add in chopped eggs with mustard, mayo, paprika, pepper, and salt. Top with green onion.
7. Lastly, serve as a side with your favorite meat dish.

Quick and Easy Idea #7: Cheesy Egg Cups

Number of people served: 4

Time you'll need: 12 to 16 minutes

Calories: 117

Fats: 8.8g

Proteins: 8.7g

Carbs: 1.8g

What you'll require:

- Eggs (four)
- Cheese (Cheddar, 125g, shredded)
- Veggies (diced, your choice, veggies tomatoes, mushrooms, and/or peppers, 221g)
- Milk (low-fat, non-sugar, 221g)
- Pepper & salt (as preferred)
- Cilantro (chopped, 125g)

What you'll require for the Topping:

- Cheese (shredded, your choice, 221g)

Also Required:

1. Jars (medium, four)
2. Water (0.5L)

What you need to do:

1. First, whisk up cheese, veggies, pepper, eggs, milk (low-fat), salt, and cilantro.

1. Next, combine the mix into each jar. Tighten lids (not too tight) to keep water from entering the egg mix.
2. Then, arrange the trivet in the Instant Pot and add the water. Arrange the jars on the trivet and set the timer for 5 minutes (high pressure). When done, quick release the pressure, and top with the rest of the cheese (½ cup).
3. Lastly, broil if you like for 2 to 4 minutes till the cheese is browned to your preference.

Quick and Easy Idea #8: Asparagus Appetizer/Side Salad

Number of people served: 4 to 6

Time you'll need: 18 to 22 minutes

Calories: 221

Fats: 8.6g

Proteins: 15.7g

Carbs: 8.1g

What you'll require:

- Red potatoes (small, 455g)
- Asparagus (fresh, trimmed and chopped lengthwise)
- Tuna (2 tins)
- Olives (Greek, 125g, pit removed)
- Dressing (Italian, low sugar, 45g)

What you need to do:

1. First, chop potatoes and let soak in water for about 5 minutes to let starch drain.
2. Next, put water in the pot, about 2 inches, and heat up to a boiling point. Throw in chopped potatoes to cook for about 12 to 14 minutes.
3. Then, in the remaining 2 to 4 minutes of cooking potatoes, add asparagus to the water.
4. After, turn off the heat, remove water from asparagus and potatoes and then place it into ice water.
5. Lastly, serve with tuna and olives as an appetizer or side for a chicken or fish dish.

Quick and Easy Idea #9: Low-carb Pork Treat

Number of people served: 4 to 6
Time you'll need: 18 to 22 minutes

Calories: 221
Fats: 8.6g
Proteins: 15.7g
Carbs: 8.1g

What you'll require:

- Pork (tenderloin, 455g)
- Salt (14.5g)
- Pepper (18.5g)
- Oil (Olive, 75g)
- Cider (apple, 95g)
- Syrup (maple, non-sugar, 25g)
- Vinegar (apple cider)

What you need to do:

1. First, set up your oven to 190 degrees Celsius.
2. Next, cut up tenderloin into two pieces or to fit in the pan or skillet you are using. Transfer into another container.
3. Then, put oil in pan, or skillet, and then fire up for about 6 to 8 minutes. Toss in vinegar, syrup, and cider while adding pepper until boiling point. Make sure to remove bits stuck to the bottom.
4. After, throw in meat. Prepare thoroughly until the mixture is reduced to glazed texture.
5. Lastly, remove and serve while adding sauce for glazing. Serve with a side of veggies.

Quick and Easy Idea #10: Easy Fish Delight

Number of people served: 4 to 6   Time you'll need: 18 to 22 minutes

Calories: 257

Fats: 8.8g

Proteins: 25.7g

Carbs: 9.2g

What you'll require:

- Breadcrumbs (low-carb, 56g)
- Oil (Olive, 45g)
- Dill (fresh, 45g, snipped)
- Salt (10.5g)
- Pepper (5g)
- Filet (tilapia or salmon, 50g per filet)
- Juice (lemon, 25g)
- Lemon (wedges)

What you need to do:

1. First, set up the oven to 186 degrees Celsius. Add the pepper, oil (olive), dill (fresh), salt, and juice (lemon).
2. Next, add filet (fish of your choice) into a baking container which has been previously coated with grease. Add breadcrumbs on top of fish patting down to so they stick. Coat both sides.
3. Then, let sit in the oven until fish is tender, roughly for 12 to 14 minutes.
4. Lastly, serve with veggies and add lemon wedges on top.

Chapter 6: Low-Carb Recipe Ideas

Low-Carb Recipe Idea #1: Balsamic Roast Delight

Number of people served: 4 to 6

Time you'll need: 35 to 40 minutes

Calories: 51

Fats: 3.1 g

Proteins: 4.5 g

Carbs: 2.3 g

What you'll require:

- Chuck roast (one, no bone, 1.5kg)
- Onion (chopped, 55g)
- Water (0.5L)
- Ground pepper (black, 14.5g)
- Garlic (powder, 14.5g)
- Salt (kosher, 14.5g)
- Vinegar (balsamic, 14.5g)
- Xanthan gum (25g)

For Garnishing:

- Fresh parsley (chopped, 20g)

What you need to do:

1. First, combine the garlic powder, salt, and pepper and spread on the meat to prepare the seasoning.
2. Next, utilize the skillet to sear the meat. Add in the vinegar and deglaze the skillet, or pan, while you let cook for another couple of minutes.
3. Then, toss in onion into a pot along with (two cups) boiling water into the mixture. Cover with a top and allow simmer for thirty to forty minutes on medium-low heat.
4. After, remove meat from pot and add to a cutting surface. Shred up into chunks and throw away any fat and/or bones.
5. Now, add in the xanthan gum to the broth and mix up briskly. Place the thoroughly cooked meat back into the pan to heat up.
6. Lastly, serve with a favorite side dish.

Low-Carb Recipe Idea #2: Burger Calzone Treat

Number of people served: 6
Time you'll need: 25 to 30 minutes

Calories: 400
Fats: 25.1g
Proteins: 24.5 g
Carbs: 2.6 g

What you'll require:

- Mayonnaise (45g)
- Onion (yellow, one diced)
- Beef (ground, 750g, lean)
- Cheese (cheddar, 75g, shredded)
- Flour (Almond, 95g)
- Cheese (Mozzarella, 75g, shredded)

- Egg (one)
- Bacon (4 thin strips)
- Dill pickle (4 spears)
- Cheese (cream, 95g)

What you need to do:
1. First, program the oven to 185 degrees Celsius. Set up a baking container with parchment paper.
2. Next, chop up pickles into lengthy spears. Set to one side when completed.
3. Then, to prepare the crust, combine half of the cream cheese and the mozzarella. Insert into microwave 30 seconds. Upon melting, add egg and almond flour to prepare the dough. Set aside.
4. After, set the beef to fire on the stove using a medium temp setting.
5. Now, cook bacon (microwave for approximately four minutes or on the stovetop with pan or skillet). Upon cooling, break up into bits.
6. Now, dice up an onion and toss into the beef to cook until tenderized. Throw in bacon, pickle bits, cheddar cheese, the rest of the cream cheese, and mayonnaise. Move briskly.
7. After that, roll the dough into a prepared baking container. Place the mixture into the middle of the container. Fold up ends and side to create the calzone.
8. Lastly, insert into until brown or about 12 to 14 minutes. Let it rest for 10 minutes before cutting up.

Low-Carb Recipe Idea #3: Steak Skillet Nacho

Number of people served: 3 to 4

Time you'll need: 26 to 33 minutes

Calories: 376

Fats: 31.5g

Proteins: 19.4g

Carbs: 6.1 g

What you'll require:

- Cheese (Cheddar, 75g)

- Coconut oil (45g)
- Butter (15g)
- Beef (Steak, round tip, 1kg)
- Cauliflower (750g)
- Turmeric (15g)
- Chili (powder, 15g)
- Cheese (Monterey Jack, 75g)

For Garnishing:

- Sour cream (25g)
- Jalapeno (canned, 20g, slices)
- Avocado (105g)

What you need to do:

1. First, set up oven temp to 176 degrees Celsius.
2. Next, prepare the cauliflower into chip-like shapes.
3. After, combine the chili powder, turmeric, and coconut oil in a mixing container.
4. Then, throw in cauliflower and add it to a container. Set the timer for 18 to 24 minutes.
5. Now, over a med-high fire in a cast iron pan, place butter. Fire up until both sides are thoroughly done, flipping only one time. Let it sit for six to nine minutes. Slice up thinly and add in some pepper and salt to the meat.
6. After that, move the florets to the pan and add in the steak bits. Top it off with the cheese and bake six to nine more minutes.
7. Lastly, serve with your favorite side of veggies.

Low-Carb Recipe Idea #4: Portobello Burger Meal

Number of people served: 4

Time you'll need: 22 to 27 minutes

Calories: 327

Fats: 23.1g

Proteins:19.4g

Carbs: 6.1 g

What you'll require:

- Mushroom (Portobello, 6 caps)
- Beef (ground, 455g, lean)
- Pepper (Black, 6g, ground)
- Worcestershire sauce (14.5g)
- Salt (pink or kosher, 12g)
- Cheese (cheddar, 56g or 6 slices)
- Oil (avocado, 12g)

What you need to do:
1. First, remove the stem, rinse, and dab dry the mushrooms.
2. Then, combine the salt, pepper, beef, and Worcestershire sauce in a mixing container. Shape into patties.
3. After, fire up the oil (medium fire). Let caps simmer about four to five minutes on each side.
4. Next, move the mushrooms to a bowl, utilizing the same pan, prepare the patties for six minutes, turn, and prepare another six minutes until ready.
5. Now, combine the cheese to the patties and cover for about a minute to melt the cheese.
6. Lastly, add a mushroom cap to burgers along with the desired garnish to serve.

Low-Carb Recipe Idea #5: Low-carb Super Chili

Number of people served: 4
Time you'll need: 20 to 24 minutes

Calories: 319
Fats: 24.1g
Proteins:39.2g
Carbs: 3.4g

What you'll require for the Chili:
- Stock (beef or chicken, 25g)
- Steak (1kg, cubed into 1-inch cubes)
- Leeks (sliced, 25g)
- Cumin (4g)
- Cayenne pepper (ground, 4g)
- Pepper (black, 4g)
- Salt (4g)
- Whole tomatoes (canned with juices, 221g)
- Chili powder (2.5g)

Additional Toppings:
- Cheese (cheddar, 221g, shredded)
- Sour cream (95g)
- Cilantro (fresh, 25g, chopped)
- Avocado (one half, sliced or cubed)

What you need to do:
1. First, toss all of the fixings into the cooker - except the toppings.
2. Then, use the cooker's high setting for about six hours.
3. Lastly, serve and add the toppings.

Low-Carb Recipe Idea #6: "You won't believe it's low-carb" Chicken Parmesan

Number of people served: 2 to 4

Time you'll need: 34 to 40 minutes

Calories: 586

Fats: 31.4g

Proteins: 55.5g

Carbs: 2.7g

What you'll require:

- Rinds (pork, 221g)
- Sauce (Marinara, 45g)
- Chicken (breast, 455g)
- Cheese (parmesan, 56g)
- Garlic (powder, 12g)
- Pepper & salt (as preferred)
- Egg (one)
- Cheese (Mozzarella, 125g, shredded)
- Oregano (12g)

What you need to do:

1. First, set up an oven temp setting of 165 degrees Celsius.
2. Next, utilize a food processor to mash rinds and cheese (parmesan). Add them to a mixing container.

3. After, pound chicken breasts until they are about one-half inch thick. Whisk up egg and dip chicken in for the egg wash. Place the chicken into crumbs.
4. Then, distribute the breasts on a lightly greased baking container evenly. Add in seasonings and insert them into the oven for approximately 23 to 26 minutes.
5. Now, cover with the marinara sauce over each serving. Top with the mozzarella and bake for 12 to 14 minutes.
6. Lastly, serve with a bed of spinach.

Low-Carb Recipe Idea #7: Tangy Coconut Chicken

Number of people served: 4 to 5

Time you'll need: 25 to 28 minutes

Calories: 492

Fats: 39.7g

Proteins:28.9g

Carbs: 2.3g

What you'll require for the Tenders:

- Egg (large, one)
- Onion (powder, 8.5g)
- Curry (powder, 18.5g)
- Pork rinds (Crumbled, 125g)
- Chicken (thighs, 1kg, no bone or skin, about 6 to 8 pieces)
- Coriander (14.5g)
- Coconut (shredded, 95g, unsweetened)
- Garlic (powder, 8.5g)
- Pepper & salt (as preferred)

What you'll require for spicy and sweet mango sauce dip:

- Sour cream (25g)
- Ginger (ground, 14.5g)
- Mango extract (15g)
- Mayonnaise (25g)
- Sugar-free ketchup (25g)
- Cayenne pepper (14g)
- Liquid stevia (7 to 8 drops)
- Garlic (powder, 8.5g)
- Red pepper (flakes, 5g)

What you need to do:

1. First, program oven to 185 degrees Celsius.
2. Then, whisk the eggs and debone the thighs. Slice them into strips (skins on).
3. Next, add the spices, coconut, and pork rinds to a zipper-type bag. Add the chicken, shake, and place on a wire rack. Bake for about 14 minutes. Flip them over and continue baking for another 18 minutes.
4. Lastly, combine the sauce components and stir well. Serve with your favorite side of veggies or salad.

Low-Carb Recipe Idea #8: Slow cook Chicken Casserole

Number of people served: 3 to 4

Time you'll need: 35 to 45 minutes

Calories: 224

Fats: 9.4g

Proteins:30.4g

Carbs: 5.7g

What you'll require:

- Chicken breasts (two in cubes)
- Bay leaf (one)
- Cheese (Mozzarella, 221g, shredded)
- Tomato sauce (256g or one tine)
- Seasoning (Italian, 14.5g)
- Salt (5.5g)
- Pepper (4g)
- Optional: slow cooker (2-quart)

What you need to do:

1. First, remove the bones from the chicken and chop it into cubes. Add them to the slow cooker.
2. Next, pour in the sauce over the chicken and add the spices. Stir and cook on the low setting for thirty to forty minutes.
3. Lastly, serve with the cheese as a topping.

Low-Carb Recipe Idea #9: Low-carb Roll Up Treat

Number of people served: 2 to 4
Time you'll need: 15 to 20 minutes

Calories: 191
Fats: 7.9g
Proteins:15.6g
Carbs: 1.9g

What you'll require:

- Eggs (large, 6)
- Milk (221g)
- Garlic (powder, 14.5g)
- Salt (kosher, 9.5g)
- Pepper (Black, 9.5g, freshly ground)
- Butter (11g)
- Chives (chopped, 5g)
- Bacon (slices, 12)
- Cheese (cheddar, 105g)

What you need to do:

- First, in mixing container, whisk up eggs together along with milk and garlic (powder). Add in salt & pepper as preferred.
- Next, in skillet or pan, melt butter over medium fire. Toss in eggs and scramble for 2 to 4 minutes. Toss in chives.
- Then, on a cutting surface, cut up bacon slices. Place cheddar on the bottom and then toss in a bunch of eggs. Roll up very closely.
- Lastly, place rolls back into pan, or skillet with the seam facing down. Remove once crispy. Serve with whole-grain toast.

Low-Carb Recipe Idea #10: Cauliflower Cheese Surprise

Number of people served: 2 to 4

Time you'll need: 10 to 20 minutes

Calories: 164

Fats: 6.5g

Proteins: 16.3g

Carbs: 2.4g

What you'll require:

- Cauliflower (one Head, about 256g)
- Eggs (two)
- Cheese (parmesan, 75g)
- Oregano (35g)
- Cheese (cheddar, 75g, shredded)

What you need to do:

- First, cut up cauliflower into individual florets. Place them into a food processor until the texture appears similar to rice. You could also grate if you don't have a processor.
- Then, in a mixing container, combine cauliflower, eggs, cheese (parmesan), and the oregano. Mix up until even and add salt & pepper.
- After, fire up a skillet, or pan, over medium fire. Todd mixture into the pan. Pat down to form a patty. Exert pressure using a spatula. Cook for 4 to 6 minutes. Turn over and repeat on the other side.
- Lastly, sprinkle cheese until it is melted. Make "sandwiches" by putting two pieces together. Serve as a snack or side to your favorite meat dish.

Chapter 7: 7-day Sample Low Sugar Diet Plan

In this chapter, we are presenting a 7-day sample plan to give you an idea of how you can put together a winning combination of healthy foods. Please bear in mind that this is only a guide. So, feel free to customize this plan as you get more experience and develop your own style.

	Week One		
Day / Meal	**Breakfast**	**Lunch**	**Dinner**
Monday	Fresh fruit bowl topped with granola and honey	Veggie and chicken club sandwich on whole wheat bread	Chicken and veggie casserole
Tuesday	Spicy breakfast burritos	Bean soup with croutons	Grilled salmon and veggies
Wednesday	Scrambled eggs, bacon and a slice of whole-grain toast	Mixed garden salad, fresh veggies, and grilled chicken	Sirloin and veggies surprise
Thursday	Low-sugar cereal with low-fat	Steak and potatoes with a	Chicken fajitas with mashed

		dairy milk	side of crispy veggies	potatoes
Friday		Veggie cheesy bits	Grilled salmon, sautéed veggies with garlic whole wheat toast	Roast beef club sandwich with crispy plantain bits
Saturday		Low-sugar whole grain flapjacks	Spicy chicken fajita burritos	Veggie pizza with small salad
Sunday		Whole grain veggie breakfast wraps	Tangy Mexican bean bowl with guacamole	Chicken noodles and sautéed veggies

www.ingramcontent.com/pod-product-compliance
Lightning Source LLC
LaVergne TN
LVHW020411070526
838199LV00054B/3578